W9-AZT-409

Kenya

Kenya

BY SYLVIA MCNAIR
AND LYNNE MANSURE

Enchantment of the World
Second Series

Children's Press®
A Division of Scholastic Inc.

NEW YORK   TORONTO   LONDON   AUCKLAND   SYDNEY
MEXICO CITY   NEW DELHI   HONG KONG
DANBURY, CONNECTICUT

Frontispiece: African elephants in front of Mount Kilimanjaro

Consultant: Dr. Michelle Gilbert, Department of Fine Arts, Trinity College

Please note: *All statistics are as up-to-date as possible at the time of publication.*

Visit Children's Press on the Internet: http://publishing.grolier.com

Book Production by Herman Adler Design

Library of Congress Cataloging-in-Publication Data

McNair, Sylvia.
    Kenya / by Sylvia McNair and Lynne Mansure.
        p. cm. — (Enchantment of the world. Second series)
    Includes bibliographical references and index.
    ISBN 0-516-21078-5
    1. Kenya—Juvenile literature. [1. Kenya.] I. Mansure, Lynne. II. Title. III. Series.
DT433.522 .M46 2001
967.62—dc21   00-065646

Acknowledgments

The authors owe a large debt of gratitude to many people who shared their knowledge and experiences with us. We must lead with Rosalie Osborn, longtime friend and retired wildlife educator. Representatives of Kenyan institutions who were especially helpful include Elmanus A. Vodoti of the Kenya Embassy in Washington, D.C; Jacinta Nzioka of the Kenya Tourism Board; Frederick Karanja Mirara, National Museums of Kenya; Terry Kantai, PRIDE, Ltd.; Irene Njumbi, Wildlife Clubs of Kenya; John Sinayi, Railway Museum; and Ali Abubakar, Fort Jesus Museum. All of the following people, in alphabetical order, helped in various ways: Said Abdalla Ahmed, Dr. Gurmeet Bambrah, Njoki Kamau, Nancy Klatt, Eric Leshao, John Mark Leshao, Konga Mbandu, Paul Muiruri, Zubeida Muiruri, and Josephat Ngonyo.

Of particular assistance in arrangements for Sylvia McNair's research trips to Kenya were Jean Walden and Lonrho Hotels, as well as British Airways, whose employees always make the long flights comfortable and enjoyable.

Contents

Cover photo:
A woman wearing traditional tribal clothing

Zebras in a national reserve

El Molo tribespeople

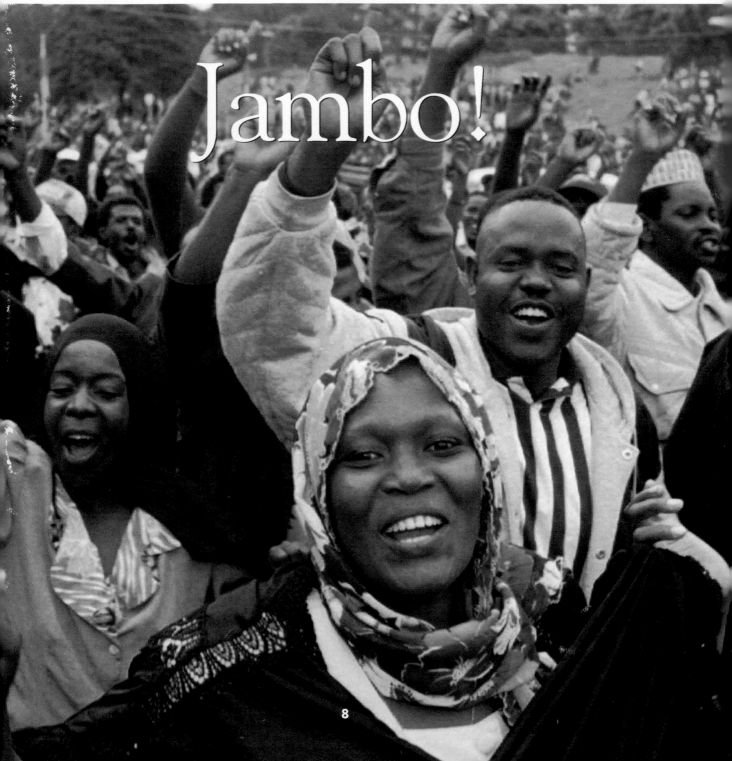

Jambo!

Statue of Jomo Kenyatta
in Nairobi

"*Jambo.* How ARE YOU?"

"I'm well, thank you. *Habari?*"

"*Mzuri. Asante.* Beautiful day, isn't it?"

Welcome to Kenya, where people speak English and Swahili and a mixture of both. Often, a few words in Arabic, Hindi, or traditional African languages are also sprinkled in.

Welcome to the land of Kenya, its snow-covered peaks and sandy beaches, its vast deserts and savannas, its fertile fields and orchards. Welcome to its cities and villages.

Opposite: **A crowd cheers as President Daniel arap Moi is sworn in for the fifth time as president of Kenya in 1998.**

Jambo! **9**

Rothschild's giraffes in Lake Nakuru National Park

Welcome to the wildlife of Kenya: the herds of elephants and water buffalo, the graceful giraffes, the lion prides, and baboon families. Welcome to the magnificent national parks and reserves where these precious animals are protected.

Welcome to the people of Kenya, who are striving to preserve their cultural heritage while living in the twenty-first century. Welcome to the farmers, the herders, the fishers, the park rangers, the technicians, and civil servants. And most of all, welcome to the children of Kenya, who would like to have you discover their beloved country.

Children planting trees

**Geopolitical map
of Kenya**

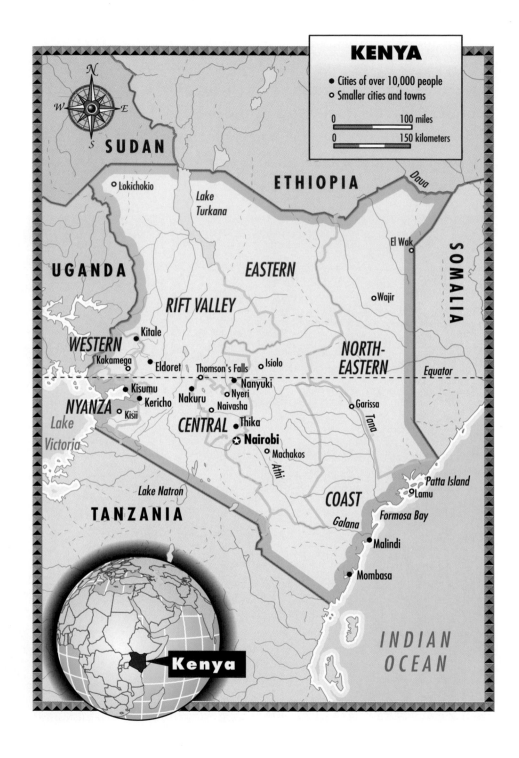

KENYA

- Cities of over 10,000 people
- Smaller cities and towns

0   100 miles

0   150 kilometers

SUDAN

ETHIOPIA

Dava

Lokichokio

Lake
Turkana

El Wak

SOMALIA

UGANDA

EASTERN

Wajir

RIFT VALLEY

WESTERN

Kitale

NORTH-
EASTERN

Kakamega

Eldoret

Thomson's Falls

Isiolo

Equator

Nanyuki

Kisumu

Nyeri

Garissa

NYANZA

Kericho

Nakuru

Naivasha

Tana

Kisii

CENTRAL

Thika

Lake
Victoria

Nairobi

Machakos

Athi

Patta Island

Lake Natron

COAST

Lamu

TANZANIA

Galana

Formosa Bay

Malindi

Mombasa

Kenya

INDIAN
OCEAN

Kenya's national motto is *Harambee*. It means "Let's pull together." After the nation gained its independence from Great Britain in 1963, Jomo Kenyatta became its first president. Kenyatta had heard longshoremen at the seacoast shout "*Harambee!*" as they loaded and unloaded ships' cargoes. He decided it would be a good slogan for the newly independent nation.

Kenyatta told the people that the only way to make a success of their new independence was for all the citizens to work together to help themselves. The use of this national slogan was new, but the principle of cooperation has always been a tradition in Kenya. When there is a problem, people get together to figure out a solution. They call *harambee* meetings to work together when needed. One day a whole group may go together to help harvest a crop; on another day they might help a member repair a house.

Harambee is also used as a slogan to raise funds to help disaster victims, such as people suffering near-starvation because of severe droughts. Kenyan children are trained from an early age to contribute money to help people less fortunate than themselves.

So welcome to Kenya, the land of *harambee*!

Jomo Kenyatta made "*Harambee*" Kenya's national motto.

The Land
of Kenya

In 1848, two German missionary-explorers sent reports back to Europe about a huge mountain towering over the plains of eastern Kenya. Its cap, they said, was covered with white snow that sparkled brilliantly in the sun. Geography scholars laughed at the story. "How can that be?" they asked. How could a country on the equator have snow? It must be a hoax or a mirage.

But the reports were true. Mount Kenya's great height, 17,058 feet (5,199 meters) above sea level, keeps its summit under a permanent blanket of snow. The same is true of Tanzania's Mount Kilimanjaro, which rises to 19,340 feet (5,895 m) just south of Kenya. Yet it is only a short journey from these frigid peaks to the hot, steamy ports and the white sand beaches on the coast of the Indian Ocean.

Temperatures and climate are affected by *latitude*—the measure of the distance from Earth's equator. In general, regions at the North and South Poles are the coldest on earth; those regions at the equator are the hottest. But *altitude*—how many feet or meters a place is above sea level—is another critical factor. The higher you go, the colder it gets.

Opposite: **A clear stream runs down from Mount Kenya through McKinder's Valley in Mount Kenya National Park.**

Palm trees provide some shade on Malindi Beach.

Kenya's Geographical Features

Area: 224,979 square miles (582,650 sq km)

Highest Elevation: Mount Kenya at 17,058 feet (5,199 m) above sea level

Lowest Elevation: Sea level along the Indian Ocean

Longest River: Tana River at 440 miles (708 km)

Largest Lake: Lake Victoria, 26,828 square miles (69,479 sq km); 1,460 square miles (3,781 sq km) located within Kenya

Largest Lake Totally within Kenya: Lake Turkana at 2,473 square miles (6,405 sq km)

Greatest Annual Precipitation: About 50 inches (130 cm) in the highlands

Lowest Annual Precipitation: About 10 inches (25 cm) in the northern plains

Highest Average Temperature: About 90°F (32°C) on the coast

Lowest Average Temperature: About 60°F (16°C) in the high plains

Greatest Distance North to South: 640 miles (1,030 km)

Greatest Distance East to West: 560 miles (901 km)

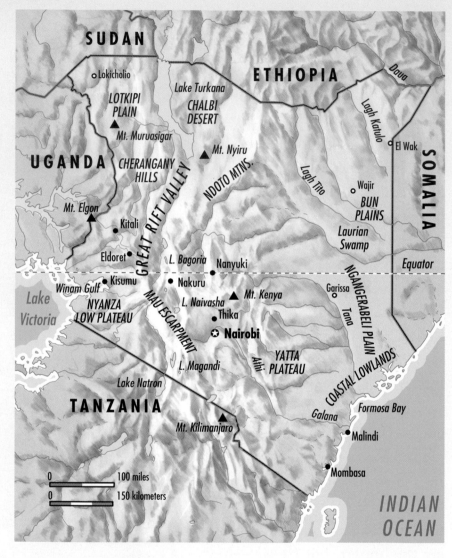

Kenya is on the equator, but it has great variations in altitude. Several plateaus of different heights rise like giant steps from the seacoast into the interior. These plateaus, along with numerous mountain peaks and deep valleys, are factors in the country's many climatic and ecological characteristics.

Hundreds of millions of years ago, the continent of Africa lay deep under ocean waters. Later, a large continent rose from the sea. Back then, the present-day land masses of South America, Antarctica, Africa, and Asia were all joined together. These continents gradually broke apart. Violent earthquakes and volcanic eruptions thrust the land of Africa upward, forming mountains and valleys. Streams running down from higher elevations created rivers and lakes. The land began to take different shapes—grasslands, forests, and

Zebras graze the savanna in Masai Mara National Reserve.

wetlands. All of this happened long before the first of Africa's great herds of animals evolved and began to roam across the plains and woodlands.

Today, about one-third of Kenya's land area is arid or semiarid. Another third is made up of highlands and has mountains, lakes, forests, and fertile farmland. The remaining third is grassland, called savanna.

The Great Rift Valley

The surface of Kenya has a huge crack—a steep-sided gash that runs from the Jordan River valley, in southwest Asia, through Egypt's Nile River valley, and on down through the continent of Africa. Called the Great Rift Valley, it is more than 4,500 miles (7,200 km) long. It can easily be seen from airplanes and high mountaintops.

In Kenya, the eastern branch of the Great Rift Valley cuts through the highlands. Its path is marked with volcanoes and a chain of seven lakes. Walls rise on either side of the valley floor to heights that range from 100 feet (30 m) to more than 4,000 feet (1,200 m). An accumulation of salts and minerals make the waters in all but two of the lakes undrinkable. Hot, saline springs bubble up around the edge of Lake Magadi (picture above), where salt, potash, and other minerals are mined.

Kenya's Location and Size

The continent of Africa is shaped like a fat comma. The equator runs through it, along a line that roughly divides the northern, broader portion of the continent from the southern, narrower part. The Mediterranean Sea, the Red Sea, and the Gulf of Aden lie along the northern and northeastern shores of the continent. The continent tapers southward to a rounded point called the Cape of Good Hope. On the west is the Atlantic Ocean. The Indian Ocean is on the east.

The Republic of Kenya is located in eastern Africa, and lies on both sides of the equator. It is a small country, a little larger than France, a little smaller than the state of Texas. It covers 224,979 square miles (582,650 sq km). Its boundaries are shared with the countries of Tanzania, Uganda, Sudan, Ethiopia, and Somalia, and with the Indian Ocean.

To the south, the Tanzania-Kenya border is mostly a straight line, running northwest from the Indian Ocean to Lake Victoria. The slopes of Mount Kilimanjaro are partially in Kenya, though the peak of this famous landmark is in Tanzania. Kenya's jagged western border starts in Lake Victoria. It extends northward along western Uganda, then veers off to the northeast along a short boundary shared with Sudan. Ethiopia lies to the north along another jagged boundary. Three straight lines form a sort of bracket that separates Somalia from Kenya on the east, and the Indian Ocean is Kenya's southeastern border.

Because all of Kenya is close to the equator, there is little difference in the length of daylight from one time of year to another. The sun travels along an almost identical path, day after day. It rises quickly in the morning, so there is almost no dawn, and sets below the horizon just as abruptly in the evening.

Temperatures vary only slightly throughout the year, but there are rainy and dry seasons. The heavy rains come during March, April, and May, then again from late October until early December.

The land of Kenya can be described in five geographical regions. Each has different physical characteristics, different natural resources, and a different climate. The Nyanza low plateau and the Kenya highlands are more heavily populated than most other sections of Kenya.

Looking at Kenya's Cities

Located in southern Kenya on the Indian Ocean, Mombasa (below) is Kenya's second-largest city and chief port. The city was a center of trade as early as A.D. 110. In the 1000s, Arabs settled in Mombasa. It came under Portuguese control in the 1500s and 1600s. From 1887 to 1907, the city was the capital of Britain's East Africa Protectorate. Today, Mombasa is a major agricultural market center, and its port exports large amounts of coffee, fruits, and vegetables. Mombasa is also a major manufacturing center, producing cement and refining oil. Tourism is an important business there, too. Fort Jesus is a stop for many visitors. Mombasa's altitude is sea level. Residents enjoy average July temperatures of 81°Fahrenheit (27°C) and average January temperatures of 87°F (31°C).

Kisumu, a port on the eastern shore of Lake Victoria, is Kenya's third-largest city. The city is at an altitude of 3,723 feet (1,135 m) above sea level. Kisumu's average temperatures vary little throughout the year. January days average 85°F (29°C), and July days average 81°F (27°C). Founded in 1901 as the railhead for the East African Railroad, Kisumu was also a terminal for the Uganda Railway and for an international ferry on Lake Victoria. Today, the ferry line is closed, few visitors come from Uganda, and the port's ships and warehouses have been abandoned. Visitors still enjoy Kisumu, however. The city is home to the Luo ethnic group, and the Kisumu Museum has exhibits about traditional Luo life.

Nakuru is Kenya's fourth-largest city and the farming capital of the Great Rift Valley. Founded in 1903 by Lord Delamere, Nakuru was first settled by English farm families. Today, Kenyans from nearby farms and cattle ranches buy supplies here. Nakuru is near several tourist attractions, including Lake Nakuru National Park, which is famous for its flamingos. Sometimes as many as 2 million of these birds are on the lake at one time. Menengai Crater rises 7,467 feet (2,276 m) just outside the park. Hyrax Hill Prehistoric Site is also outside the town. Since 1926, the Leakeys and other archeologists have excavated the site.

The Nyanza Low Plateau

The Nyanza low plateau is part of the Lake Victoria basin. Lake Victoria is the world's second-largest freshwater lake. It is so large that it creates its own weather system. Kenya shares access to the lake with Uganda and Tanzania.

The region around Winam Gulf enjoys year-round rainfall and fertile soil. Fishing is an important occupation. Lake Victoria is famous for Nile perch and the delicious tilapia fish. Kisumu is the area's major city.

The Kenya Highlands

The highlands of Kenya are the heartland of the country. The soil is fertile, the region gets more rainfall than most other areas, and the temperature is generally moderate and pleasant. The middle of the day may be quite hot, but the air suddenly turns chilly—even cold—as soon as the sun goes down.

The highlands are split down the middle, from north to south, by the Great Rift Valley. Mount Kenya, a giant extinct volcano, is the most dramatic feature east of the valley. The Aberdare Range, while not as high as Mount Kenya, has peaks that rise up to more than 12,000 feet (3,600 m). South of the Aberdares is some of the richest farmland in the world.

The Great Rift Valley and highlands

The Mau Mountains form the western wall of the valley. Mount Elgon, on the Kenya-Uganda border, is an impressive 14,178 feet (4,321 m) high. Its peak is snow-covered from time to time, but it does not have a permanent snowcap.

Nairobi, the nation's capital, and several other large towns are in the highlands. Cultivated fields appear near the urban sprawl. Beans, maize (corn), millet, and fruits and vegetables are grown on small farms; large-scale plantations produce tea, coffee, and flowers. Kenya is the world's fourth-largest exporter of cut flowers.

The Semidesert Regions

Much of northern Kenya and some southern areas are very dry. More than half the total land area of the nation is hot, arid territory. Droughts are frequent and the semidesert soil is very poor, making it unsuitable for agriculture. Few people live there. Those who do are herders who raise cattle, goats, sheep, and camels. These animals graze on herbs, dwarf shrubs, and the few trees that are found there.

The Yatta Plateau was formed by one of the world's longest lava flows. The Athi River runs along its base. The plateau rises abruptly from a flat plain in the southern sector of this semidesert region and extends for 190 miles (306 km). Its long, flat top is visible along much of the highway and railroad that connect the cities of Mombasa and Nairobi.

The Eastern Plateau

A narrow plateau lies between the Kenya highlands and the low-lying lands near Kenya's ocean coast. The plateau extends

People gather rainwater for drinking, cooking, and washing. Even where water is piped in, the supply depends ultimately on rain.

Much of Kenya also depends on water to manufacture hydroelectric power for lighting and to run machinery. During times of drought, rationing of electricity and sudden power outages are common problems.

The government is trying hard to provide enough water to the citizens of Kenya. Wherever possible, water is brought to a village and sold to people at distribution kiosks (see below). In rural areas, people form groups to manage water projects.

Water Problems

Water, water everywhere. During the heavy rains in Kenya, this is indeed the case (see above). But for most of the year, almost all of the country suffers from too little water. The Lake Victoria basin is the only region that usually has plentiful rain.

Many Kenyans have to make a lot of effort to get enough water for basic needs. In the arid north, it is often necessary to travel with camels and donkeys for very long distances. Young men move around with the herds in search of water. In some urban areas, they deliver water for a living, drawing it from wells and kiosks and loading it onto carts that hold a dozen or more large cans. The young men pull the carts by hand or, if they can afford it, use donkeys. In many other communities it is the duty of women and girls to fetch water for the family.

Rain is a blessing in Kenya. Grazing pastures turn green, and the livestock can get enough to eat and drink. Gardens and cash crops depend on the rains; lack of rain results in widespread drought and famine.

from the foothills of Mount Kilimanjaro northward through the Taita Hills. In most of this area, not enough rain falls to support crops. The soil is thin and poor, and very little grows except desert grass. Few people live in this region.

The Coastal Lowlands

Kenya's coastal lowlands adjoin the Indian Ocean and extend northward about halfway along the Somalia border. Offshore islands and coral reefs are part of this region. For the most part, temperatures range from hot to hotter, and humidity averages about 70 percent. The scenery along the coast is like that of tropical islands in other parts of the world, with palm trees waving in the warm ocean breezes.

The soil in the lowlands is fairly rich, and rainfall is usually adequate. Twice a year, heavy monsoons blow in off the Indian Ocean. Monsoons are a mixed blessing. Crops depend on the rain, but sometimes the lands are flooded—roads are wiped out and newly planted crops are destroyed. Crops raised in the lowlands include kapok, sisal, maize, coconuts, potatoes, mangoes, oranges, and other fruits and vegetables. Fish from the ocean is a staple part of the diet.

A view of the coastal lowlands

What's in a Name?

When European explorers traveled across the east African countryside, they arbitrarily and arrogantly bestowed European names on landmarks they saw, paying no attention to the names already used by the African people. The Europeans assumed it was their privilege to choose names in honor of their own people. Many of the European names that appeared on maps during the colonial period have now been dropped in favor of the traditional African names.

One explorer, a Scotsman named Joseph Thomson, traveled at length through the highlands in the 1880s. He named the Aberdare mountain range in honor of the president of the Royal Geographic Society, which had commissioned his trip. He also bestowed the name Thomson's Falls on both a village and a beautiful cascade (pictured at right) in the area. The mountains are still most commonly called the Aberdares, but the town, one of Kenya's highest communities, has reverted to the name *Nyahururu*, which means "where waters run deep."

The builders of the railroad from Mombasa to Lake Victoria called the town on the lake Port Florence, for the wife of one of the railroad's engineers. It is now Kisumu, Kenya's third-largest city.

Austrian explorers named a lake they saw in honor of the crown prince of Austria. Lake Rudolph is now called Lake Turkana. Lake Hannington, named for a

missionary bishop who was murdered in Uganda, is now Lake Bogoria.

But Lake Victoria is still known around the world as the namesake of Queen Victoria, who ruled the British Empire for more than sixty-three years.

The city of Mombasa is blessed with a fine deepwater port, Kilindini Harbor. Mombasa attracted traders from many lands long before outsiders ventured into Africa's interior.

Born Free

Kenya's proudest asset is its wildlife. Few places in the world have such a concentration of rare and unusual creatures roaming freely through their forests and across their savannas.

In earlier days, a hunting safari in Africa was a popular pastime for wealthy and powerful people. They hired large numbers of Africans to carry their gear and help spot the prey. Their aim was to kill rare animals and take home the animals' skins or stuffed heads as trophies.

Opposite: **A lion walks slowly along a field.**

In 1895, hunters display a lion that they killed during a safari.

Today, Kenyans recognize the unique value of these rare animals, and hunting them has been banned. Now, both residents and tourists like to go on safaris just to spot, observe, and photograph the wildlife.

The Big Five

Among the hundreds of different species found in Africa, the so-called Big Five were the most prized by hunters. The elephant, rhinoceros, lion, buffalo, and leopard were the trophies most coveted. However, many hunters didn't mind killing a lot of smaller animals while looking for the big ones.

Tourists today also hope to spot each of the Big Five. Elephants, lions, and buffaloes are usually easy to find; the rhino is less common. Sighting a leopard is extremely difficult. They are not only rare; they are also very wary and are almost never seen during the daytime. Leopards are solitary animals that defend their own territory even from other leopards. Mother leopards take care of their cubs for two years after birth.

A black rhino in Masai Mara National Reserve

Joy Adamson and Elsa

Joy Adamson was an Austrian woman who lived in Kenya for forty-three years. While there, she married George Adamson, a game warden, and the couple adopted a lion cub that they named Elsa. Elsa grew up with them as a beloved pet, and even after she had been released into the bush, she made several visits to her "foster parents." On one of those visits, she brought her three young cubs and showed them off to her human friends.

Joy wrote a book about Elsa called *Born Free*. It has been translated into twenty-five languages and has been read by at least 70 million people. The movie by the same name was equally popular. The story of Elsa has had a worldwide impact on people's interest in and understanding of animal behavior.

Joy gave lectures about Elsa and wildlife conservation in many other countries. She helped establish four national parks in Kenya and helped people in other countries to do the same.

Joy was also a talented artist. She made hundreds of detailed drawings and paintings of Kenya's flora

and fauna, which were very useful to scientists. She also painted many fine portraits of African men and women, most of them wearing traditional clothing and adornments.

Joy was murdered in 1980, but her work lives on in her paintings, her books, and the cause of wildlife conservation. A movie about George and Joy Adamson, *To Walk with Lions*, starring Richard Harris and Geraldine Chaplin, was released in 1999.

The lion is large, powerful, and beautiful, but it really doesn't deserve the title "King of the Beasts." Both elephants and buffaloes can defeat lions in a contest.

Currently, the most endangered of the Big Five is the rhinoceros. Rhinoceroses travel in families or small groups. Illegal hunters, called "poachers," kill the massive, usually gentle rhino not for meat but just for its horn, which has great value in markets in other parts of the world. Rhino horns are used to make knife handles in some non-African countries; they are ground into a powder for so-called medicinal purposes in others.

The Grazers

Easier to find and delightful to watch are giraffes, zebras, and many species of antelopes. These creatures are vegetarians. They usually travel in large herds and are active during daylight hours. They're also easy to spot because they graze in open plains and lightly wooded areas.

Giraffes—with their long, graceful necks—eat leaves from treetops that are out of reach for most other creatures. There are three types of giraffes in Kenya. The reticulated giraffe has sharply defined white markings on its red-brown coat. The Rothschild giraffe, found in Lake Nakuru National Park, has white "stockings" on its legs. The most common giraffe is the Masai giraffe.

At the Giraffe Center, southwest of Nairobi, tourists can feed and photograph the animals close-up. Safari drivers report that with tourists, giraffes are the most popular of all Kenyan wildlife.

A reticulated giraffe with its calf

An Elephant Orphanage

There is a very special orphanage on the grounds of Nairobi National Park called the Sheldrick Center. Baby elephants that have lost their mothers—usually because they were shot by poachers—have been cared for here since the 1970s. An orphaned baby elephant doesn't know how to survive when its mother dies. It reacts much as a human baby would—staying by the mother's side and grieving. If not rescued, it will eventually die of starvation and, some say, a broken heart.

A baby elephant feeds every few minutes. It lives exclusively on mother's milk for its first two years—and continues to need some milk until it is five years old. In the past, orphans rescued by park rangers always died because no suitable infant formula had been found. Daphne Sheldrick, wife of the founding warden of Tsavo National Park, worked for a long time to develop a successful formula for the baby elephants. Today, a laboratory in England manufactures the formula and donates it to the orphanage.

Workers feed and care for the baby elephants at the orphanage, working in shifts around the clock. The employees do not handle the same creatures every day, because it is not good for the animals to become too attached to individual humans. Eventually, the young elephants must be ready to join and bond with herds of wild elephants. Visitors are allowed to watch the babies each day when their keepers take them to a special place for a mud bath.

When the babies are old enough to eat some grass, they are transferred to Tsavo National Park. There they join the older orphans who arrived before them. It is true that elephants have good memories—they happily recognize old friends when they are reunited. Some years later, as a teenager, each elephant will leave its younger friends behind and begin adult life in the wild. All of the orphans have been given names, and park rangers spot them from time to time and send news of their activities back to the orphanage.

Occasionally, other orphaned animals are kept for a short time at the Sheldrick Center. Recent inhabitants included a baby zebra and an infant rhino named Makosa (Swahili for "mistake").

The Sheldrick Center is named for the late David Sheldrick, whose widow continues to direct the work of the orphanage.

Gazelles in the rain

Antelopes come in all sizes. The regal eland, with its distinctive spiraling horns, is the largest and heaviest. The impala is the highest jumper, and the topi—recognizable by the patches of black on its thighs—is the fastest. Wildebeests (also known as gnus), hartebeests, waterbucks, and many species of gazelles are all part of the antelope family.

The oryx has a horselike body, black-and-white facial markings, and long, straight horns. The bongo is a rare species of antelope that lives in wooded areas. A large animal, it is a rich chestnut brown in color, with thin, white, vertical stripes.

An endangered bongo in the Aberdare Range

The zebra is sometimes called a "horse with striped pajamas." Its Swahili name is *punda milia*, which actually means "striped donkey." Thousands of zebras live on Tanzania's Serengeti Plain and travel with the wildebeests into Kenya during an annual migration. All the grazers—zebras, giraffes, and antelopes—live peaceably together in open grasslands and lightly wooded areas.

Cats and Other Carnivores

All members of the cat family are carnivores—they live on meat. Most of these predators know instinctively how to hunt and kill their prey. Cheetahs are an exception—mother cheetahs have to teach their young how to hunt.

Lions look like huge, cuddly pussycats, but they are rightly feared by smaller animals. Female lions take care of their cubs for two years after birth. Several lionesses usually live together with their cubs and a few adult males. The family group is called a *pride*. Cubs regard all the females in the pride as their mothers. The males are nomadic and don't stay with the family indefinitely.

Lionesses hunt as a group; cheetahs usually hunt alone. Cheetahs eat only freshly killed animals. Other cats are scavengers and will eat leftover meat

A cheetah scampers up a tree in Masai Mara National Reserve.

A dwarf mongoose pauses at its den entrance on a termite mound.

of animals killed by other creatures. Leopards and several smaller, somewhat rare cats also live in Kenya—the African wildcat, golden cat, caracal, and serval.

Hyenas, jackals, foxes, and wild dogs are also carnivorous. Several small, weasel-like animals—mongooses, civets, genets, zorillas, and otters—live on eggs and small living creatures.

Primates

Several species of primates live in Kenya. Most common is the vervet monkey, sometimes called the green monkey. These animals are very active and noisy. They live in large family groups with lots of youngsters. They are slight, agile, long-tailed, and mischievous. Other monkeys in Kenya include the colobus, which inhabits highland forests, and several types that live in savanna country.

A female baboon carries her baby on her back.

Baboons are heavily built monkeys. Two types of baboons live in Kenya. Named for their coloring, they are known as yellow baboons and olive baboons. They live in very large family groups made up of both sexes and all ages. Baboons make their homes in wooded areas and sleep at night. They are so numerous in some parts of the country that a member of Parliament once complained that he had more baboons than people in his area!

On a Photographic Safari

Most tourists to Kenya have one desire above all others—to go on a safari, or journey. In earlier days, the object was to kill big game, but that is no longer permitted. Today's tourists are armed only with cameras. Drivers transport passengers to areas in national parks and game reserves where animals congregate. The drivers are experienced spotters, and they know about the habits of different species. Each game drive is different, but here are some examples.

It is almost sundown. Along the edge of a stream in Amboseli National Park, a hundred or so water buffalo are walking in a long line. Hiding in the bush on the other side of the stream are two lions. They are wary, careful not to make a move that might call attention to them.

Lions are no match for full-grown buffaloes. But these two lions are waiting patiently in the hope that a baby buffalo will fall behind the herd. Then they'll have a chance to grab their supper.

Far to the north, in Samburu National Reserve, three reticulated giraffes are browsing for their dinner. The level grassland is dry and brown, dotted with brush and acacia trees. Here and there are tall mounds of dirt; these are termite homes. Large nests built by weaver birds hang from the branches of an acacia tree. From a distance, the nests look like dozens of large, dark, coconut-shaped fruits.

The tallest giraffe is the mother, and the other two are her youngsters. They are eating the leaves of the acacia trees, gracefully moving from one to another. Mother giraffe watches carefully, making sure her youngsters are getting enough to eat. She's also protecting them from danger. Each time a driver inches his vehicle a little closer, the mother moves in between the car and her children.

In another part of the reserve, two young male giraffes are "necking." They nudge each other with their long necks, but sometimes the nudge is more of a light blow. They are tussling, engaging in a playful fight, just as two human boys might do.

It is early morning in Masai Mara. The sun is just appearing over the horizon. Even here, near the equator, it is very chilly. Drivers have spotted something the viewers will want to see. Several vehicles take off at a fast clip, all heading for the same spot. They pull up at the edge of a savanna, a few yards from a clump of trees.

A beautiful, sleek cheetah has found and killed a delicious young bushbuck, a small striped antelope with twisted horns. The fascinated tourists watch and snap photo after photo. The cheetah pays no attention to the people. His mind is on his food.

The passengers in the van are not the only spectators. A few vultures are flying overhead, and a hyena peeks out of the woods. Guinea hens trot around nearby, searching the ground for seeds. Several monkeys are scrambling around in the trees, overlooking the scene. They are chattering loudly, trying to persuade the cheetah to go away. He ignores them, too.

Somehow, the sight of a cheetah devouring another animal does not seem disgusting or cruel. It is simply a normal part of nature.

Mother and baby hippopotamuses by the Mara River

Hippopotamuses share Kenya's lakes and rivers with many kinds of fish. Hippos spend all day floating and lazily bouncing

up and down in the water, usually in groups. At night they swim away from their favorite pools and come on land to find food, which consists mostly of very short grasses. In spite of their great size—up to two tons or more—their effortless lifestyle ensures that they do not need a great deal of nourishment. Hippos are dangerous to humans who get in their way on land or water. They can easily tip over boats or run over people in their path.

Crocodiles inhabit Kenya's freshwater lakes and rivers, and there are many varieties of snakes, both poisonous and non-poisonous, in marshy areas. The nation has more than 180 species of lizards of various sizes. There are three species of tortoises and one kind of freshwater turtle.

Sport fishing is good on Lake Naivasha. Families who live near Lake Turkana are able to support themselves by fishing, and deep-sea fishing off the coast is outstanding. Marlin, tuna, swordfish, and Pacific sailfish are all abundant.

Coral reefs and gardens, as well as colorful tropical fish, attract divers and underwater photographers to the coast of Kenya.

Reptiles on Display

Mamba Village, outside Mombasa, is the largest crocodile breeding farm in Africa. *Mamba* is the Swahili word for crocodile. Here, visitors can watch the reptiles and learn about their lifespan and habits. Crocodiles are raised commercially for their meat and their hides. They can live to a very old age—from 120 to 180 years. Beginning at age 12, the female is able to produce eggs for as long as she lives.

The National Museums of Kenya in Nairobi has a Snake Farm, where all the snake species native to Kenya are kept in glass cages. There are several species of vipers, cobras, and other venomous snakes. Snakebites can cause death, and Kenyan children who visit the Snake Farm learn about the snakes and how to avoid them. Lizards and turtles are also on display, and there is a small greenhouse.

Adult and chick ostriches at Masai Mara

Pink flamingos at Lake Nakuru

The ostrich is the largest bird in the world, and Kenya has many of them. Ostriches cannot fly, but they can run as fast as 45 miles per hour (72 kph). Their legs are powerful enough that one kick can kill a person. They lay eggs that measure about 6 inches (15 cm) long. Ostriches run around the savannas and are commonly seen by visitors on safaris.

Several other birds spend most of their time on the ground and are large enough to be recognized easily. These include the secretary bird (so named because its head feathers resemble feathers once used to make quill pens), the gorgeous crowned crane, the great white heron, the marabou (a stork), and large colonies of white pelicans. Vultures often glide overhead, looking for meat to scavenge.

From a distance, Lake Nakuru often looks like a pink sea. Up to 2 million brilliant flamingos sometimes congregate there.

As for smaller birds, more than 1,200 species have been recorded, and naturalists believe there are many more that have not yet been identified. As many as 6 billion migratory birds visit Africa from far northern lands each year.

Kenya's varied geography offers habitats for birds who like mountains, swamps, forests, or desert. During rainy seasons, when the lands along the rivers turn green and lush, the trees are full of nesting birds.

Plant Life

The acacia, or umbrella thorn tree, dots the savanna landscape of Africa. These trees are usually seen standing apart from one another by at least several yards. The acacia's trunk is not very large, but its branches spread out in a wide, umbrella-like shade. More than forty species of acacias are native to Kenya. Giraffes like to eat the leaves of the acacia, and impalas browse for fallen seed pods.

A most unusual Kenyan tree is the baobab. Unlike the acacia, the baobab's trunk is fat—as wide as 30 feet (9 m) in diameter. But its branches are almost scrawny and have no

National Parks, Reserves and Monuments

National Parks	National Reserves	Monuments
1 Aberdare	A Arawale	a Gedi Ruins
2 Amboseli	B Bisa-Nadi	b Olorgasaaillie
3 Central Island	C Boni	
4 Hells Gate	D Dodori	
5 Kora	E Kerio Valley	
6 Lake Nakuru	F Kiunga	
7 Meru	G Lake Bogoria	
8 Mount Kenya	H Losai	
9 Nairobi	I Malindi Marine	
10 Ol Doinyo Sabuk	J Marsabit	
11 Tsavo East	K Masai Mara	
12 Tsavo West	L North Kitui	
13 Ruma	M Rahole	
14 Saiwa Swamp	N Samburu	
15 Sibiloi	O Shaba Springs	
	P Shimba Hills	
	Q South Kitui	
	R South Turkana	

Bamburi Nature Trail

An empty limestone quarry outside of Mombasa has been transformed into a beautiful nature park. The land was once beneath the Indian Ocean, but the water receded millions of years ago and left a deposit of rocky, barren, coral soil.

In 1950, a cement plant was built here, and the company began production in 1954. Bulldozers and excavation machinery scooped up the coral limestone from a 750-acre (304 hectare) quarry. The coral was some 17 to 33 yards (16–30 m) deep, reaching down below sea level. Pools formed at lower levels. About four times a year, the Indian Ocean experiences huge tides. The effect of the tides cause a rise and fall in the partly salty quarry pools.

When it was no longer profitable to dig limestone from the quarry, the government asked permission to use the big hole as a dump. Instead, the Bamburi Cement Company decided to invite a noted Swiss agronomist (an expert in crops and soils) named René Haller to see what he could do with the big hole in the ground.

Haller planted twenty-six species of trees. The saltiness of the water and shallowness of the roots killed most of them. But a few did well—notably the casuarina tree, from Australia. The casuarina tree drops its needles, which are eaten by small insects. Gradually, the process of needles falling and insects dying created a layer of humus—a fertile material made up of partially decomposed plant and animal matter.

As some trees flourished and the soil built up, monkeys and birds came to live in the park. They brought in seeds of fruits and other plants, and their droppings introduced additional plant life. Eventually, a timber forest grew over the sterile limestone.

Giant tortoises from the Seychelles were brought in. They eat grass and keep the place neat. Eland, oryx, poultry, and farm animals were added. Today, crocodiles are bred and released here. Integrated agriculture includes cocoa, rice, and bananas, and the park now has Kenya's largest freshwater fish farm.

Bamburi Nature Trail has been recognized as one of the most successful environmental projects in the world.

leaves during much of the year. Although they do not look particularly healthy, baobab trees live to be hundreds of years old. Elephants tear off their bark and chew it; owls and bats sometimes live in hollows in their trunk. Some tribal legends tell of spirits living in baobab trees.

Many palms and tropical flowering trees were introduced to Kenya centuries ago by early traders. Mangrove forests, one result of these plantings, thrive in coastal regions. Thousands of species of flowers and other plants flourish in Kenya's forests, deserts, grasslands, and wetlands.

A flowering tree in the Great Rift Valley

From Prehistory to Independence

42

THE EARLIEST ANCESTORS OF ALL HUMANKIND MAY HAVE been living in Kenya's Great Rift Valley more than 2 million years ago. Archeologists have been finding fossilized remains of early hominids (humanlike creatures) in East Africa ever since the 1920s. Their discoveries have given the region a nickname—the "Cradle of Mankind."

Not much is known about the lifestyles and habits of these early ancestors of modern humans, but scientists have gathered a wealth of materials to study. Replicas of some of the most important archeological discoveries are on display at the National Museums of Kenya in Nairobi. According to current theories, there were two types of hominids some 2 million years ago—plant-eaters and meat-eaters. These species existed before the development of *homo erectus*, a species much like modern humans. A nearly complete skeleton of this species, that of a twelve-year-old boy, was found near Lake Turkana in 1984.

Hominids evolved into modern, intelligent humans over hundreds of thousands of years. By about 20,000 years ago, the

Opposite: **The silhouette of a tree and Masai tribal members as the sun begins to rise**

Fossilized remains of early hominids have been discovered in East Africa.

inhabitants of the East African landscape were hunter-gatherers who made crude tools. Various nomadic people came into the area several thousand years ago.

By A.D. 130, an Egyptian geographer named Ptolemy had mapped the Kenyan coast. Written history starts around A.D. 900, when Islamic Arabs began trading with people who lived in the coastal settlements. Over the next few hundred years, Arab and other travelers began to migrate to the coast of East Africa and to develop trade routes to the interior. A culture we now call *Swahili* developed along the shore of the Indian Ocean. Nearly all Swahili people are Muslims; the religion was spread through conversion and intermarriage. The Swahili language comes from the Bantu family of cultures, but it includes many borrowed words from other tongues.

The Portuguese Influence

In the years before and after A.D. 1500, many European explorers were sailing the globe. Among the most active explorers were the Portuguese. The coastal areas of East Africa had already been exposed to the cultural, political, and economic influences of Arabs, Indians, and other migrants and travelers from the East. The European influence began in 1498, when the Portuguese sea captain Vasco da Gama arrived in present-day Malindi after sailing around the Cape of Good Hope. He found a pilot there to help him continue on his way to India.

The Portuguese established a fort in Mombasa and built up a lively trade in gold, ivory, and slaves. Their dominance of the East African coast lasted for about 200 years, then became

Two Historic Sites

In Gedi, a historic site a few miles south of the coastal city of Malindi, are the ruins of an Arab-African, or Swahili town founded around A.D. 1400. A walled city covering about 45 acres (18 ha), it was occupied off and on for the next 300 years. Excavations have revealed a palace, a grand mosque (a place for worship), several stone houses that indicate the inhabitants were prosperous, and a large tomb.

Construction of Fort Jesus in Mombasa (pictured above) was begun in 1593 by Portuguese explorer-traders. The fort is a major landmark overlooking the old port of the city. Exhibits in the fort provide a valuable overview to the history of coastal Kenya and of the Swahili culture. The people of the coast belong to nine villages, or tribes, of Bantu-speaking peoples with a common historical and cultural heritage. Collectively, they are called the *Mijikenda*.

Both Gedi and Fort Jesus are administered by the National Museums of Kenya. Guided tours are available for tourists.

undermined by diseases such as malaria and bubonic plague. Eventually, the local Swahilis, who had always resented the Portuguese rule, called on their fellow Muslims and trading partners, the Arabs of Oman, to help them drive out the invaders. Their efforts succeeded. By the early 1700s, the Portuguese had left the Kenyan coast for good, and the Omani Arabs took over as the rulers.

For the next century and a half, the coast of Kenya was under Omani Arab rule. Large plantations were established in the region to furnish food to Oman and supply goods for trade. The wealthy Arab settlers used slaves to produce rice and other grains, fruits, and coconuts. In 1832, the Omani ruler transferred his headquarters to Zanzibar, an island off the coast of Africa.

The Interior

Meanwhile, European nations were becoming interested in the interior of the African continent. Unlike the coastal regions, where outsiders had been visiting and intermixing for centuries, the highlands and deserts to the west were largely unknown to the rest of the world. The territory was rural, and people lived in small groups of extended families, or clans. Councils of elders governed the clans. Many different languages were spoken, some of them closely related to one another.

People survived by hunting, gathering, herding, and raising crops. Trade was conducted through a barter system. In general, people believed in one supreme being, but each community practiced its own religious rites and traditions.

British and German missionaries, explorers, and merchants began to visit and claim large parts of East

Illustration showing missionaries teaching some members of the Zanzibar people

Africa during the mid-1800s. In 1886, Great Britain and Germany agreed to divide up the region. Germany would run the area called Tanganyika, and Britain would rule over what is now Uganda and Kenya. According to an agreement with the sultan of Zanzibar, a 10-mile (16-km) strip of the Kenyan coast became a British Protectorate. The sultan's representatives continued to handle a number of matters. Nearly a century later, in 1964, Tanganyika and Zanzibar would unite to create the Republic of Tanzania.

British Colonialism

European imperialism carved up the continent of Africa during the late nineteenth century. Three motives drove the movement—economic, religious, and political. Most Europeans truly believed that they had a God-given right to seize control of many lands inhabited by people they considered "uncivilized." They would convert the natives to Christianity, take over their lands, and introduce modern methods of agriculture. No matter that the native tribes had their own cultures, systems of government, and economic practices—the Europeans thought they were fulfilling the "destiny" of white Christians to rule over "inferior" people and change their way of life.

A company called the British East Africa Association was incorporated under a royal charter in 1888 to develop the area. When the task became too large due to financial concerns and political turmoil, the British government took over, establishing the British East Africa Protectorate in 1895.

Governors were appointed by the Colonial Office in London. At first the government operated from Zanzibar, and later from Mombasa. In 1920, the country was renamed the Kenya Colony and Protectorate.

The Lunatic Express

The British Parliament decided in 1885 to build a railway from Mombasa to Kisumu, on Lake Victoria. This would open up the interior of East Africa for travel, trade, and colonial settlements. Opponents in Parliament thought the plan would be disastrously expensive and called it "a lunatic line to nowhere." They did not succeed in stopping the scheme.

Work began in 1896, the first rail was laid a year later, and the line reached Kisumu five years later. It was a huge task, costing millions of British pounds and requiring thousands of workers.

In the nineteenth century, workers construct a railroad.

Railroad officials tried to recruit local workers to build the railroad. Few Africans were interested, so the company imported thousands of construction workers, as well as some surveyors, from India. The hilly terrain in the interior made the task difficult, and heavy rains washed away miles of embankments. Workers faced extremely hot weather near the coast and bitterly cold conditions in the mountains. Hundreds of them died of malaria and other diseases.

Allidina Visram

The story of Allidina Visram is one of rags to riches. As a young man of fourteen, he found his way from India to Zanzibar in 1877. He had no money or contacts and very little education, but he managed to survive and, eventually, to prosper.

Allidina met a trader who hired him to do odd jobs. He soon learned how to calculate in currencies from different localities. He could trade in Indian rupees, coins from Zanzibar, and even in cowrie shells, which were sometimes used as currency. He also knew how to barter, trading such goods as ivory, silk, cotton, and guns.

From other traders, Allidina heard exotic tales of tribal lands in the African interior. Fascinated, the young man dreamed of becoming successful in the unknown territory. He and a cousin walked for forty days, carrying trade goods into the interior. The trip earned them some profits, and he used his share to open a store. Soon he opened several more.

When the British started building the railroad, Allidina traveled to present-day Uganda. Over the next few years, he established stores in many parts of East Africa and became successful and rich. The British government often followed his lead and set up offices in places where Allidina had a store. The British encouraged Africans to plant crops, which Allidina bought.

Always fair with the Africans, Allidina paid good prices for their produce and for the products they made. He loaned money to the settlers to start their farms, running each of his stores as a sort of savings bank. As World War I was approaching, Allidina sold off his properties in German territory and moved his headquarters to Mombasa.

Allidina Visram is honored as one of East Africa's trailblazers. A statue of him stands in Mombasa's Treasury Square, and a high school in the city is named for him.

The railroad was responsible for many changes, including the growth of the city of Nairobi. Before the railroad came, Nairobi was a small, swampy little community. In 1907, it became the capital of the colony.

White Settlements

When the railroad was finished, the British could easily travel to the interior of East Africa. They found a vast, fertile land that appeared to be sparsely populated. Many of the British dreamed of establishing a white, English-speaking colony like those that had been formed in the United States, Canada, and Australia.

In the highlands, groups of Masai tribespeople lived a nomadic lifestyle, using the pastures for their herds during different seasons. There were also Bantu tribes who lived and planted crops on the hillsides and used the plains for grazing and hunting. To the white settlers, the land seemed to be comparatively empty. They were eager to take over the fertile fields and establish farms. Thus a large region in the heart of Kenya became known as the White Highlands.

In 1915, the British passed the Crown Lands Ordinance, which declared that only white people could legally own land. The Africans were expected to live in the so-called native reservations.

Up until that time, Africans lived off the land and didn't have much use for money. The settlers needed to hire workers to help them run their large farms, but they found it hard to recruit Africans. So the colonialists created a need for money by imposing taxes on the natives and encouraging Asian traders to open stores where the Africans could buy such attractive items as beads, cloth, and blankets. Many young men found it necessary to leave the farms and move to towns in search of paid employment.

Traditionally, rule by councils of respected elders was the norm among the tribes. The colonial administrators, however, wanted to have direct control. They selected willing local people to serve as chiefs, or headmen, of the villages and tribes. These new leaders had to enforce the white colonials' policies.

Life got worse for the Africans during World War I. The British were fighting battles against the Germans in the neighboring country of Tanganyika (now Tanzania). Africans were recruited into the British army, where they served as porters. Thousands of them lost their lives, and even more died from famine and diseases soon after the war ended.

A photo taken about 1917 shows Africans who were pressed into service by the British during World War I.

An economic crisis after the war brought new problems. Wages to native workers were lowered, and new privileges were handed to the colonials. A "Soldier Settlement Scheme" offered farm parcels in the highlands to the white war veterans.

In 1920, the name of the colony was officially changed to the Kenya Colony and Protectorate. When Africans protested, the English answered with military force. Kikuyu tribespeople brought suits against them, arguing points in tribal law, but the English courts always decided in favor of the white settlers.

The Leakey Family

The Leakeys, a family of European descent, are among the most famous Kenyans of the twentieth century. Louis Leakey (pictured) was born in Kenya in 1903, the son of British missionaries. While still a teenager, he became interested in archeology and led expeditions to hunt fossils in eastern Africa.

After World War I, Louis went to school and university in England. He graduated in 1926 and returned to Africa for more archeological work. In 1936, he married Mary Douglas Nicol. Over the years, they discovered fossils many millions of years old in East Africa. Louis Leakey's discoveries—along with those of his wife and his son Richard—literally rewrote theories of the origin of human beings. The Leakeys' writings offer evidence that the very first people on earth lived in what is now Kenya.

The Leakeys had three children. Jonathan, a naturalist, has specialized in snakes and in the development of anti-snakebite medicine. Philip was the first white man elected to Parliament by the African majority, and he was later appointed a government minister. Richard has been active in archeology, politics, and wildlife conservation.

Rumblings of Discontent

Harry Thuku is recognized as Kenya's first national hero. A member of a wealthy Kikuyu family, he knew how to read and write English. He had a government job in Nairobi but was secretly seeking ways to protest the poor treatment of Africans. Members of the Indian community in Kenya were asking for more equality, and Thuku was inspired by their efforts.

On June 10, 1921, Harry Thuku founded the Young Kikuyu Association (YKA). The organization opposed several government policies: the takeover of native lands by colonial settlers, high taxes, low wages, and the law forcing all blacks to carry an identity card at all times. Soon a larger organization was formed to take in members of other tribes besides the Kikuyus. This was the East African Association (EAA).

Thuku and his organization became more and more open about their grievances. On March 14, 1922, the government arrested him. The arrest of this popular hero caused an immediate reaction—a general strike. Thousands of Africans gathered in Nairobi to protest.

The government retaliated with force. Shots rang out and fifty-six protesters were hit. Twenty-five of them, including four women and one child, were killed. Thuku was exiled to a remote village in the desert. Around the world—even in England—people were shocked at the massacre. The colonial governor was replaced. But before long, the EAA was ordered to disband.

Protesters immediately reorganized, this time calling their group the Kikuyu Central Association (KCA). Another young man, then known as Johnstone Kenyatta, was emerging as a leader. The KCA worked underground to improve the lives of black Kenyans through establishing independent schools and a Kikuyu-language newspaper. Kenyatta was an eloquent speaker, and he encouraged Kikuyu pride.

In 1929, Kenyatta was sent to England to plead for the rights of the Indian community—as well as for the rights of Africans—in colonial East Africa. Kenyatta spent the 1930s and half of the 1940s abroad, but he would return later to carve his name in Kenya's history.

The colonial government made some halfhearted attempts to appease the discontented Africans. Local native councils were established in 1925. Commissioners, chiefs, elders, and young leaders of transtribal associations got together to discuss their concerns. Unfortunately, they could do nothing much besides talk.

World War II

War broke out in Europe in 1939. The British colonial government banned all African political associations and arrested several of their leaders. At the same time, Africans were recruited into the British army. These black soldiers served in Kenya, Ethiopia, India, and Burma. Their fighting experience made many of them determined to assert their rights when they got back home.

The colonial government had made a few concessions, including the appointment of Eliud Mathu to the legislative chamber in 1944. Mathu had organized a political organization called the Kenya African Study Union (later shortened to Kenya African Union, or KAU).

By 1946, Jomo Kenyatta—as Johnstone Kenyatta now called himself—was internationally famous as an activist and the author of a best-selling book, *Facing Mount Kenya*. He returned to his native land to head the KAU as the most important voice of the Kenyan people.

Mau Mau

As the KAU grew in strength, there were several confrontations between Africans and the British authorities. A strike supported by the KAU in Mombasa was ruthlessly suppressed. During another strike, authorities shot down nine workers.

A few Kikuyu ex-servicemen formed a secret society known as the Mau Mau. The group's primary objective was to get the Europeans out of the country and put the Kikuyus in control. Frustrated with the British refusal to recognize the rights of Africans, the Mau Mau quickly became a terrorist organization. It was officially outlawed in 1950, but more and more Kenyans—not all of them Kikuyu—joined the movement. Soon there were an estimated quarter of a million members. A new governor was sent out from England in 1952. He declared a state of emergency that lasted for five years.

Kenyatta was not a part of the Mau Mau, but the government didn't trust him. Police stormed his home on October 20, 1952, and he surrendered peacefully. Five other leaders of KAU were arrested, then dozens more. Heads of African religious groups and trade unions were rounded up first, then thousands of others. The trial of Jomo Kenyatta went on for five months.

When the state of emergency was declared, the Mau Mau leaders who favored an armed struggle moved into the forests of Mount Kenya and the Aberdares. Thousands of young men, eager to fight, followed them. The fighters were given military training, and some learned to make homemade guns. Many swore never to cut their hair until the country gained independence.

Mothers, sisters, and wives of the fighters brought food to the forests for them. To stop the delivery of food, the government soon forced women and children to live in villages

In 1953, members of the Kikuyu tribe were held in a prison camp during the Mau Mau conflict.

surrounded by barbed wire. They were compelled to work at such jobs as building roads and were only allowed to return to work on their own farms for a couple of hours a day. Family members of well-known freedom fighters were held in prisons or detention camps. More than 100,000 Kikuyu were arrested. A state of martial law was in effect—civil rights did not exist. Much of the government's budget was spent on prisons and police.

The Mau Mau did commit acts of terrorism, but retaliation from the government resulted in the loss of many more lives. The Mau Mau were responsible for the deaths of 32 white civilians and 167 security officers. More than 13,000 Africans were killed, some by the government and some by the Mau Mau. The government also hanged some 1,000 Africans.

Independence at Last

Independence movements were gaining ground all over the world. Public opinion in England and other countries was turning against colonialism. In Kenya, elections were held for representatives to the legislative council in 1957. The KAU, renamed Kenya African National Union, became a legal political party. Kenyatta, still in prison, was elected its president.

All over Kenya, the motto was proclaimed: *Uhuru na Kenyatta*, "Independence (Freedom) with Kenyatta." The national hero was set free in 1961, and 30,000 Kenyans gathered to welcome him back. On his release, Kenyatta immediately went to work to bring the divided Kikuyu community together.

On December 12, 1963, the British flag was lowered for the last time. The black, green, and red national flag of Kenya was raised as a symbol of the nation's independence.

Before that date, people visited the forests to inform the last of the freedom fighters that the goal they had fought for had been achieved. People attending the ceremonies were thrilled to see the longhaired men of the forest celebrating along with the rest of the crowd in the stadium.

Jomo Kenyatta waves to a crowd as he arrives in Nairobi.

Uhuru!
Independence!

KENYA HAS HAD ONLY TWO PRESIDENTS SINCE IT BECAME independent in 1963. At first, skeptics in the outside world did not have much faith in the ability of Kenyans to work together and create a stable society. Then, as Jomo Kenyatta continued to be the nation's leader for fifteen years, critics said, "Well, what will happen when Kenyatta dies? Then Kenya will fall apart." But when Kenyatta died in 1978, his vice president, Daniel arap Moi, peacefully and legally succeeded him as president. And while the nation faces many serious problems, thus far Kenya has been one of the most stable governments in Africa.

Kenyatta set out to modernize the nation without violating tribal and religious traditions. He worked to bring equal status under the law to all classes and tribes. In spite of the racial bitterness that had preceded independence, he invited the white settlers living in Kenya to stay. He knew that Kenya's economy would need foreign investments in order to thrive.

Kenyatta wanted an undivided, nonracial nation. He brought opposing factions and members of different tribes into the government. The first vice president was a leftist leader, Oginga Odinga. Tom Mboya, a moderate who had campaigned for independence, was minister for economic planning.

Tom Mboya

Tom Mboya (far right in photo) was thirty-three years old when Kenya became a nation. He had already been active in the international union movement and in politics for a dozen years. After studying politics, economics, and industrial relations at Oxford University in England, his union work had allowed him to travel widely and meet many world leaders.

Mboya helped write the Constitution for the new government and was widely recognized as one of Kenya's most promising young leaders. Tragically, his life was cut short at the age of thirty-nine when a gunman assassinated him on a street in Nairobi.

Kenyatta was a great and successful leader, but he was also a dictator who dealt harshly with his enemies. He and his family amassed a huge fortune during his fifteen-year rule. At the same time, Kenya was in many ways democratic. There was only one political party of any significance, but general elections were held every five years. The government supported a free press, public schools, and public health services.

The Nyayo Period

Kenya's second president, Daniel arap Moi, ascended to the office upon Jomo Kenyatta's death in 1978. In honor of Kenyatta, President Moi proclaimed a new national slogan, *Nyayo*, which means "to follow in the footsteps." Under Moi, educational and public health facilities and services expanded greatly.

Jomo Kenyatta

Jomo Kenyatta was the first president of the newly independent nation of Kenya. A brilliant, charismatic, and complicated man, he formed a working democracy out of people from more than forty ethnic groups. He united them under the slogan *Harambee*—"Let's pull together."

Kenyatta was born around 1895. His parents called him *Kamau wa Ngengi* (Kamau, son of Ngengi). His people had little contact with the white settlers in surrounding regions.

Kamau became very sick when he was ten years old, and his parents took him to the white people's hospital near Nairobi. He recovered and went home, but he never forgot the missionary doctors. He was also curious to learn more about the world outside his village. Before long, he ran away from home, back to the mission. He said he was an orphan and asked to stay.

A fast learner, Kamau quickly learned English and mastered several useful skills. He missed his own people, however, and returned home. He went through the Kikuyu coming-of-age ritual and got married. Before long, he drifted back to the mission. The teachers gave him a new English name—Johnstone Kamau.

When he was in his twenties, Kamau went to live in Nairobi, which was now the capital city of the colony. He got a government job and decided to change his name again, to Johnstone Kenyatta. *Kenyatta* is the Kikuyu word for a white, red, green, and black beaded belt, which he wore for much of his life to remind himself of his origins.

Kenyatta kept a foot in each world—he respected Christianity and the white culture, but he also wanted to help preserve Kikuyu traditions. He started the country's first Kikuyu-language newspaper. He became a powerful public speaker, in English and Swahili as well as in his native Kikuyu. He quit his job and became secretary of the Kikuyu Central Association.

The Indian community in Kenya sent Kenyatta to England in 1929 and 1931. He stayed until 1946. He studied many subjects, traveled abroad, and became known as an activist—a busy public speaker and petition writer. He also published two widely read books. After a while he dropped the English name Johnstone and called himself Jomo Kenyatta.

From 1946, when he returned to his homeland, until his death, in 1978, the story of Kenyatta's life is completely merged with the history of Kenya.

Kenyatta's life had many fascinating chapters. He was married four times and had several children. He changed his name several times as he went through life. But he probably appreciated the nickname "Mzee" most of all. That is what his followers called him during his last years. It means "old one" or "wise one," and is a term of love and respect.

Richard Leakey

Richard Leakey, son of famous Kenyan archeologists Louis and Mary Leakey, was born in 1944. He discovered an important fossil when he was only six years old. As an adult, he became interested in many other aspects of Kenyan life, especially conservation.

Leakey became the director of the National Museums of Kenya in 1968. In 1989, he took over as director of the Wildlife Department of the Ministry of Tourism and Wildlife. He continued as director when the department became an independent agency in 1991. Leakey raised large amounts of money for the Kenya Wildlife Service (KWS) and is credited with much of the country's success in attracting tourists to view its wildlife. Under his leadership, poaching of elephants and rhinos decreased, and the population of these species began to rise.

An outspoken and often controversial person, Richard Leakey was forced to resign from KWS in 1994. He cofounded a new political party, *Safina* (The Ark). After the 1997 elections, he was appointed to Parliament by his party. In 1998, he resigned his office to become head of KWS once again. In 1999, President Moi appointed Leakey to the post of secretary to the cabinet and head of the public service.

Voters in Nairobi

There has been political turmoil in Kenya under Moi's leadership. In 1982, members of the Kenyan Air Force tried to overthrow Moi's government, but they were unsuccessful. Moi succeeded in hanging on. The first multiparty elections were held in Kenya in 1992. President Moi was reelected that year, and again in 1997.

Kenya faced serious economic problems in the 1990s. An economic crisis started in 1993, and heavy rains caused by El Niño resulted in devastating floods in 1997 and 1998. A bridge on the Nairobi-Mombasa road—Kenya's most important artery—collapsed during the Christmas season. The two cities were cut off from each other, and thousands of travelers were stranded.

Inflation soared, tourism dropped off, and unemployment reached catastrophic heights. The economic problems caused increased crime, especially in the cities. According to many experts, there was also widespread corruption on the part of some government officials.

A Terrorist Attack

August 7, 1998, was a day of horror in Nairobi. News reports rapidly sent emotional shock waves around the world. Bombs had simultaneously destroyed the U.S. embassy buildings in the capital cities of Kenya and Tanzania. The attack, planned by international terrorists, was meant as a blow against the United States, but its effect on the people of the two African cities was disastrous.

The devastation in Nairobi was especially widespread. Inside the embassy, 32 Kenyans and 12 Americans were killed. In surrounding areas, the explosion killed 213 others. More than 5,000 people were injured, most of them severely enough to need hospital treatment.

The embassy was completely destroyed. About forty other buildings in the heart of the city were damaged. One seven-story building caved in from the shock waves, killing more than 60 people.

A school bus carrying 45 youngsters was passing in front of the embassy when the blast occurred. Miraculously, all of the passengers survived.

Crowded *matatus*—vans operated as privately owned buses—transported hundreds of people to hospitals, where many of them were treated free of charge. Nairobi's major newspaper, the *Daily Nation*, credited many ordinary people with helping to save hundreds of lives. The Kenya Medical Association and twenty-three other organizations set up a program called Operation Recovery to assist survivors.

Governmental Structure

Kenya is a constitutional republic, with three branches of national government—executive, legislative, and judicial. For many years, it was a one-party state, dominated by Jomo Kenyatta's Kenya African National Union (KANU). In 1991, it became a multiparty system again.

The executive branch is headed by a president, who is elected by popular vote for a five-year term. President Moi is not eligible, under the Constitution, to run for re-election in 2002, but there have been reports of attempts to change that restriction. The vice president and members of the cabinet are appointed by the president. The cabinet consists of the attorney general and the heads of more than twenty ministries. The number of ministries changes frequently.

The legislature, called the National Assembly, has 224 members. Most of them—210 members—are elected by plurality vote from single-seat constituencies; 12 are nominated by their respective parties. The other 2 are the attorney general and the speaker of the assembly. The speaker is elected by a two-thirds majority of the other members.

Nine political parties elected representatives to the legislature in 1997. The majority were members of KANU.

NATIONAL GOVERNMENT OF KENYA

Executive Branch

PRESIDENT

VICE PRESIDENT

CABINET MINISTERS

Legislative Branch

NATIONAL ASSEMBLY

Judicial Branch

HIGH COURT

COURT OF APPEAL

JUDICIAL SERVICE COMMISSION

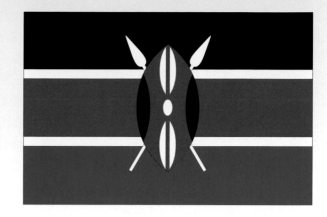

The courts, independent of the National Assembly and the executive branch, resolve disputes and interpret the law. The Constitution provides for the establishment of the High Court and appointment of its judges, a Court of Appeal, subordinate courts, Islamic courts, and the Judicial Service Commission.

Traditional Courts

When Europeans first came to eastern Africa, most of them did not understand the way tribal societies were organized. They did not realize that there were systems in place for running the affairs of the community.

Internationally, the most famous ethnic group in Kenya is the Masai. They live on both sides of the border between Kenya and Tanzania. The Masai are a small group compared to many others, but they have retained their traditional ways more than most.

A Masai community is governed by a group of elders who enforce tribal laws and sit in judgment when there are disputes. In criminal cases, the participants may choose which court will decide the case—a government court or the local traditional court.

The National Anthem

Kenya's national anthem was composed just before the country won its independence. The music is from a Pokomo (a Bantu ethnic group) lullaby.

> O God of all creation,
> Bless this our land and nation,
> Justice be our shield and defender,
> May we dwell in unity, peace and liberty.
> Plenty be found within our borders.
>
> Let one and all arise,
> With hearts both strong and true,
> Service be our earnest endeavor,
> And our homeland of Kenya, heritage of splendor,
> Firm may we stand to defend.
>
> Let all with one accord,
> In common bond united,
> Build this our nation together,
> And the glory of Kenya, the fruits of our labor,
> Fill every heart with thanksgiving.

Punishment for law-breaking is always the payment of a fine—in cattle. Cattle are a measurement of wealth among the Masai. The payment is given to the victim or victims of the offense. If an individual cannot pay the fine alone, his clan will assist him. An offender is also given counseling afterwards. Masai justice concentrates on rehabilitating the criminal and compensating his victims rather than on punishment.

Telling the truth is very important to the Masai. It is believed that a person will suffer terrible misfortune for lying. Therefore, it is assumed that people are telling the truth in court.

Kenyan Muslims follow Islamic law (*sheria*) in matters pertaining to marriage, family, and inheritance. An Islamic court has a judge (*kadhi*), but no assistants or lawyers. Two parties present their sides of the case, with witnesses to back them up. When the kadhi has heard both sides, he quotes the relevant verses of the Koran (the Muslim holy book) and gives his verdict, which is final. However, the kadhi has no legal power to enforce his verdict. In cases of disputes over property, the parties still have the option to take their case to a government court.

Nairobi: Did You Know This?

Nairobi, Kenya's capital and largest city, is the center of the country's industry and commerce. It is located in south central Kenya, in the highlands. The city is about 5,500 feet (1,600 m) above sea level. Originally founded as a railroad construction camp in the late 1890s, Nairobi became the capital of Kenya in 1963. A major part of the city's economy is tourism, based on nearby Nairobi National Park, a noted game reserve within the city limits. Industries in Nairobi include food processing, metal fabrication, and textile manufacturing.

Population: 2,143,254

Average Daily Temperature: 65°F (18°C) in January; 60°F (16°C) in July

Average Annual Rainfall: 39 inches (99 cm)

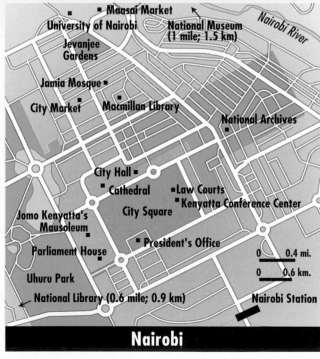

A Masai chief explains
a ritual to warriors at
a ceremony.

Local Government

For administrative purposes, the country is divided into eight provinces—Central, Coast, Eastern, North Eastern, Nyanza, Rift Valley, Western, and Nairobi area. Each is governed by a provincial commissioner appointed by the president. Each province is also divided into districts, administered by district commissioners. Chiefs and assistant chiefs are local officers of the government.

Daniel arap Moi

Daniel arap Moi has been president of Kenya since 1978. He succeeded to the presidency when Jomo Kenyatta died and has won the office during every presidential election since then.

Moi was born in a village in the Rift Valley in 1924, while the country was still under British colonial rule. His tribe is one of several ethnic groups that are known as the Kalenjin. Moi was well educated and worked as a schoolteacher from 1946 to 1955.

Along with other young men of his time, Moi was active in the independence movement. He left teaching for politics and was appointed to Kenya's Legislative Council. In 1957, he won an elected seat to the council. Moi was soon recognized as the spokesperson of the Kalenjin minority groups. He helped to found a moderate political party called the Kenya African Democratic Union (KADU). Most of the Kikuyu and the Luo supported a rival, more radical party, the Kenya African National Union (KANU).

After independence was won and Jomo Kenyatta became the new nation's first president, KADU merged with KANU. Kenyatta appointed Moi to the post of minister for home affairs. Three years later, Kenyatta also appointed him to the vice presidency. Moi served both posts for eleven years, until he rose to the presidency. President Moi has authored two books—*Kenya African Nationalism: Nyayo Philosophy and Principles* and a collection of speeches, *Which Way Africa?*

They appoint unpaid community leaders called village elders. Kenya's system of local government is based on the one established by the British colonial government.

International Relations

Kenya is a member of the United Nations and has served on the U.N. Security Council. The nation also belongs to the Organization of African Unity and several other international organizations. Kenya has embassies in thirty-four countries and consulates in five.

A crowd greets Kenya's and Japan's ambassadors to the United Nations.

Making a Living

THE KENYA AFRICAN NATIONAL UNION (KANU), Kenya's major political party, describes its philosophy as African socialism. It is based on two African traditions: political democracy and mutual social responsibility. If everyone contributes to the development of the country and increased prosperity, then everyone can share in the results. With this goal, the economy can be a mix of public and private enterprise.

Opposite: **Workers harvest sugarcane.**

Agriculture

Agriculture is the backbone of the Kenyan economy. Less than one-fifth of the nation's land is suitable for farming, yet farm products make up two-thirds of the nation's exports. Seventy percent of the workers in Kenya are engaged in agriculture.

People picking tea

Colonial settlers changed the face of Kenya's farmlands. The Europeans modernized agricultural methods, and Kenya became a leading producer of tea and coffee. This is still true today, although fluctuating prices on the world market cause problems for growers.

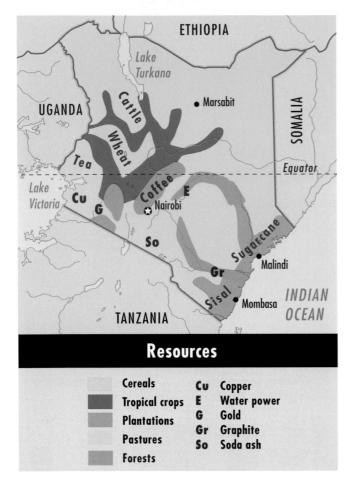

Resources

Cereals	Cu	Copper
Tropical crops	E	Water power
Plantations	G	Gold
Pastures	Gr	Graphite
Forests	So	Soda ash

Before independence, only about 4,000 settlers—almost all of them Europeans—ran the large-scale farms in Kenya's fertile White Highlands. They produced most of the grains, meat, and dairy products that were shipped to overseas markets.

The settlers were worried that the newly independent government would seize all their holdings. Some of the large estates belonging to white settlers were, in fact, bought up by the government and divided into small parcels for African families. The former owners could continue to live in Kenya if they wished, however.

After this initial forced redistribution, President Kenyatta announced that from that time forward, land would change hands on a voluntary basis, a system of "willing buyer, willing seller." In some cases, people formed cooperative societies to buy land.

A number of large ranches, as well as coffee and tea plantations, were left intact and not split up. Today, they are owned by groups that include both local and multinational investors.

Kenya has a well-developed dairy industry, with several competing companies producing yogurt, cheese, and other milk products. Most of the dairy producers are small-scale farmers.

Some beef cattle are reared on ranches, but most of Kenya's beef comes from the marginal areas of Masailand and northern Kenya. Herdsmen drive their cattle to major towns for slaughter, or middlemen bring them in trucks. If the main cattle-producing areas had refrigerated facilities, Kenya could become a major exporter of beef.

A herdsman with his cattle

Fruits, vegetables, and flowers are exported to Europe, North America, the Middle East, and Japan. Some are sent by air; others are taken to a large refrigerated facility in Mombasa and shipped out from there by boat. Mombasa is also a major port for handling goods from other African countries. It is a center of international trade, just as it has been since Arab and other traders first sailed the Indian Ocean hundreds of years ago.

The port of Mombasa

What Kenya Grows, Makes, and Mines

Agriculture (1996)

Sugarcane	4,810,000 metric tons
Corn (maize)	2,223,000 metric tons
Cassava	860,000 metric tons

Manufacturing (1994) *(valued added in Kenyan pounds)*

Food products	639,000,000
Machinery	233,000,000
Beverages and tobacco	190,000,000

Mining (1995)

Soda ash	218,450 metric tons
Fluorspar	80,230 metric tons
Salt	71,400 metric tons

Fish caught in freshwater lakes—principally Lake Victoria—are an important part of the Kenyan economy. Kenya recently fulfilled the standards for exporting fish to the European Union.

People work in a food processing factory in Nairobi.

Other Economic Sectors

After agriculture, other important sectors of the Kenyan economy are manufacturing, commerce, tourism, and government services. Industrial exports include petroleum products, cement, pyrethrum (an insecticide made from dried flowers), soda ash, and a kind of mineral called fluorspar. Important manufactured goods include

Kenyan Money

Money in Kenya is based on the Kenyan shilling. Coins are issued in denominations of 1, 5, 10, and 20 shillings, plus a 50-cent piece. The coins have an image of President Moi's head on one side and the national coat of arms on the other.

Paper notes come in values of 20, 50, 100, 200, 500, and 1,000 shillings. All of them have the same pictures on the front. A portrait of President Moi is prominent, along with the coat of arms on one side and a small circle. When held up to a light, the outline of an elephant appears in the circle. Kenyan landmarks are pictured on the reverse side of the bills.

A picture of the Moi International Stadium is on the 20-shilling bill. The 50-shilling bill displays giant sculpted elephant tusks—the symbol of Mombasa—on the left and a desert scene with a line of camels on the right. The Nyayo Monument is on the 100-shilling bill, and the Uhuru Monument and a small picture of tea pickers appear on the 200-shilling bill. The National Assembly building is featured on the 500-shilling bill. A mace shown on the left of the building symbolizes the Parliament; on the right is the traditional shield and spears from the national flag and coat of arms.

The 1,000-shilling bill, showing several animals and a bird, honors Kenya's most unique and precious asset—its wildlife.

textiles, processed foods, chemicals, pharmaceuticals, and goods made of leather, rubber, plastics, and metals. Kenya also has a major motor vehicle assembly plant.

Tourism and Conservation

Wealthy Europeans and other foreigners have been visiting Kenya for more than a century, attracted by the coastal beaches, the magnificent scenery, and the drama of safaris into the bush. Tourism exploded after Kenya won its independence and has been a major source of foreign exchange ever since. Comfortable

Mitumba

Large quantities of secondhand clothes, called *mitumba*, are sent to Kenya from other places, including the United States. People buy them both in stores and from street vendors. Customers welcome the opportunity to get decent clothes for very low prices.

The Kenyan textile industry does not like this practice at all, understandably. When a textile company goes out of business, its management blames *mitumba*, and the employees who consequently lose their jobs are quite resentful.

lodges have been built in and near game reserves and national parks. Luxury cruise ships dock regularly at the port of Mombasa.

Tourism is a very important part of Kenya's economy. From time to time, events and situations have discouraged tourists from coming. In recent years, political and economic crises, fear of terrorism and crime, and reports of disastrous floods or droughts have kept tourists away. Yet travel to Kenya is a unique and wonderful experience, especially the safaris for wildlife viewing. Not many places are left in the world where people can see so many awe-inspiring animals—some of them quite rare—in their natural environment.

Richard Leakey, a founder of the Wildlife Clubs of Kenya, has worked hard to make sure the country's wildlife is protected. This organization of schoolchildren has grown to include thousands of members. Through these clubs and his administration of the Kenya Wildlife Service, Leakey has worked hard to educate the Kenyan public about the economic value of conservation. Destruction of Kenya's marvelous wildlife population would be a disaster for the whole world, but its impact on Kenya would be especially damaging.

Ivory

Ivory elephant tusks have been a prized commodity on the international market for centuries. Ivory has been sold all over the world and carved into jewelry, knife handles, and various trinkets. Unfortunately, elephants were becoming in danger of extinction because of the ivory trade. If tusks were used only from elephants who die of natural causes, that would not be a problem. But most of the ivory comes from elephants who are shot for the sole purpose of cutting off their tusks.

Kenya has been a leader in a movement to convince people in other countries not to buy ivory. In 1989, President Moi took a dramatic step to demonstrate Kenya's opposition to the commercial use of ivory. He lit a fire that burned a total of twelve tons of ivory tusks. Another four tons were burned two years later, and twelve tons more were burned in 1995. These tusks represented millions of dollars of value on the black market.

Ivory burning is a festive occasion in Kenya. Conservationists and members of the Wildlife Clubs attend the ceremonial bonfires. Almost everybody wears a T-shirt printed with a slogan such as "Save our Elephants," "Support the Ban," or "Ivory Kills. Don't Buy It." The event is a signal to the whole world that Kenya will not tolerate the use of ivory as a commercial commodity.

UNEP and NGOs

Nairobi is the headquarters city of the United Nations Environment Program (UNEP). A beautiful $30 million complex 10 miles (16 km) north of Nairobi houses UNEP, the United Nations Center for Human Settlements (Habitat), and certain other UN agencies and programs. About 3,000 people work at the complex.

Another vital part of Kenyan society is the work done by many organizations funded by foreign groups. The term NGOs—which stands for all kinds of nongovernmental organizations working on charitable, educational, and development projects—is a familiar part of the language in Kenya.

While official Kenyan policy has been solidly behind conservation of the nation's wild animals and their habitats, this can be a very controversial issue. Farmers find it hard to appreciate wildlife that destroys crops and domestic animals. Killing wildlife is illegal in Kenya, but sometimes people take matters into their own hands, in defense of their lives and property.

The Kenya Wildlife Service tries to help people living near wildlife preserves to profit from tourism. Residents are encouraged to set up small lodges, establish craft shops, and lead

Tourists can buy traditional crafts and other items at outdoor markets.

tourists on walking safaris, with the assistance of the KWS. The organization also uses some of the income from tourists to support community projects, such as building new schools and clinics.

In spite of these efforts, the conflict between people and animals is especially obvious in Nairobi. The human population is exploding, and new residential areas encroach on lands that have been the traditional migration routes of huge herds of animals. There is great fear among conservationists that Nairobi National Park will inevitably cease to be open to migrating animals. The day may come when, instead of a great national park, it will be just a huge, fenced-in zoo.

Jua Kali

Many people in Kenya are skilled in certain kinds of work but can't find jobs. The unemployment rate is very high, so people have to find ways to make a living on their own. Some of them start small, independent businesses. For example, a mechanic repairs machinery, a carpenter builds a shed or a piece of furniture, a tailor or seamstress repairs clothing, and so on. This part of the national economy is called the "informal sector," as opposed to businesses operated by large companies or the government. Its Swahili name is *jua kali*.

Tailors work in Mombasa.

A band performs at this café.

Jua kali literally means "hot sun," because most of these enterprises start outdoors, with no fixed place of business. A worker will go from house to house or office to office with a few tools, eager to find something to fix, mend, or build. A little later he or she might build a small shack to work in, by the side of a road. These temporary structures are sometimes destroyed by authorities. But jua kali is an important part of Kenyan society and the nation's economy. A 1999 survey found that 2.4 million Kenyans are employed in the informal sector, making up more than 18 percent of the nation's gross domestic product. Recognizing the importance of this, the government sometimes builds special sheds for the use of jua kali workers.

Another form of self-employment common in Kenya is street entertainment. Jugglers, musicians, mimes, and other performers draw good-sized crowds. Many onlookers contribute a few shillings to the entertainers. Some performers also put on their acts in bars and restaurants.

Public transportation in Kenya's towns and cities is provided by *matatus*. These are privately owned minivans that operate like buses along regular routes. Owners decorate them with brightly colored pictures and designs and play loud music to attract customers. Matatus are very inexpensive, travel at high speeds, and are frighteningly overcrowded. As one Nairobi resident says, "We hate them, but we can't live without them."

Cooperatives

Much of the Kenyan economy—nearly 50 percent, according to some estimates—is controlled by cooperatives, or coops.

Harambee

Harambee is more than the national slogan—it is an organizational principle of Kenyan society and essential to the economy. The Moi administration has defined it as the idea of "assistance, joint effort, mutual social responsibil- ity, and community self-reliance. It is applied in day-to-day life in such areas as collective neighborhood house-build- ing, cultivation, irrigation, harvesting, school-building construction, construction of clinics, and fund-raising."

People make traditional handicrafts.

One outstanding example is the Akamba Handicraft Cooperative in Mombasa. Founded in 1963 by a man named Munge, the coop has some 3,000 members today. Munge actively recruited members, who could join the cooperative for a fee of 5 Kenyan shillings (less than U.S.$1). The craftspeople produce all kinds of souvenirs and artifacts made of ebony, rosewood, teak, mahogany, quinine, and mango wood. The trees are cut in government-owned forests, and steps are taken to assure that only easily replenished wood is used. Wood carvings make up about 90 percent of the total output of the Akamba Handicraft cooperative.

All cooperatives of artisans belong to the Kenya Crafts Cooperative Union. They are registered with the government and are required to hold annual meetings.

Credit Unions

PRIDE, Limited (which stands for Promotion of Rural Initiatives Development Enterprises) is a Kenyan nongovernmental organization, or NGO. It is actually a group of credit unions. PRIDE has more than 6,000 clients. It is one of a number of very small institutions that help people help themselves. PRIDE lends money and provides counseling and advice on good business practices.

People can obtain loans for use in small businesses by forming groups and becoming members of PRIDE. No one needs to pledge property as collateral because the group guarantees repayment. To qualify, a borrower must first have saved at least a little money.

Typical small businesses assisted by this type of credit include tailoring, dry cleaning, beauty salons, bicycle repair, and the sale of charcoal, groceries and housewares (above), and second-hand clothes. Initial loans are usually for $150.

Once this is repaid, an applicant can ask for a larger loan. The system, practiced widely throughout the Third World, has helped thousands of formerly poor people run successful businesses.

Kenyan women have a tradition of working together in organizations (below). They are active in social welfare, educational, and health service programs. While land titles are still held mostly by men, about 88 percent of Kenya's small farms are run by women.

An informal method of credit practiced mainly by women is called the "merry-go-round." Each member pays a small sum of money each month to her club. The money is given to a member to start a business, buy equipment, or pay unexpected medical bills. In some cases, the money is used for the community. For example, the money that is collected might be used to buy a village rainwater tank.

Kenyans Today

H OW DO YOU DESCRIBE A KENYAN PERSON?

His skin color may be of any shade—palest white, light tan, brown, or black. She may be wearing a T-shirt and blue jeans, a smart business suit, a *kanga* (a simple wraparound cotton sarong), or a silk sari. Her head may be covered with a black Muslim veil or an elaborate hairstyle of cornrows; he may be wearing a beaded or embroidered cap or an intricately twisted turban. Two Kenyans may be carrying on a conversation in English, Swahili, or any one of several dozen other languages.

And all of these people, no matter what their appearance or language, could be Kenyan citizens whose families have been here for generations. While Nairobi and Mombasa also have frequent visitors from all continents, most of the people seen in those cities, no matter what their skin color, are native-born Kenyans.

About 97 percent of the Kenyan people are of African origin. The remaining 3 percent trace their ancestry to immigrants from other parts of the world. In everyday

Opposite: **A scene in downtown Nairobi**

Women in Nairobi

Asians in Kenya

Asians from present-day Pakistan and India traveled to the coast of eastern Africa as early as a thousand years ago. They engaged in trade, and some of them settled there. Their influence is found in artifacts and architecture. Many of the Asians who live in Kenya today are descended from workers recruited by the British to build the railroad.

Asian Kenyans were active in the struggle for independence. A number of them had achieved success in business, but the British Africans discriminated against them, just as they did the native tribes.

Today, Asian Kenyans represent only a small percentage of the total population. They live primarily in the cities and larger towns, where many of them are prominent in commerce, manufacturing, and such professions as law, medicine, engineering, and teaching. They represent a variety of religions—Hinduism, Islam, Jainism, Sikhism, and others.

It is estimated that there are more than fifty subgroups of Asians living in Kenya, many of them fourth- or fifth-generation residents. They cherish the particular culture of their various backgrounds while taking an active role in the business and social concerns of today's Kenya.

speech, people are commonly spoken of as Africans, Europeans, Asians, or Arabs. Whites are called Europeans, whether their people came from Europe, North America, or Australia. The term *Asian* usually refers to people whose ancestors migrated from the Indian subcontinent. Arabs are descended from any of the nearby Arab countries. Some people whose ancestors came from an Arab country like to call themselves Arabs, even if they are of mixed blood; others prefer to refer to themselves as Swahili.

Language

Kenyans of African descent represent many different ethnic groups who migrated from other parts of Africa over time. Early Africans were primarily nomadic. They moved from place to place in groups, or tribes. They lived by hunting and gathering food, and later by herding and planting. For much of the time, individual tribes lived in relative isolation from other groups. For this reason, dozens of different languages developed. Scholars have grouped the many African languages spoken in Kenya into three divisions—Bantu, Nilotic, and Cushitic.

The nation has two official languages, English and Swahili. All teachers must know both these languages. Swahili is widely used throughout the country. Since Swahili is also spoken by many Africans in neighboring countries, it is an important vehicle for international communication, as is English.

Who Lives in Kenya?	
Kikuyu	18%
Luhya	14%
Luo	12%
Kalenjin	11%
Kamba	10%
Other Africans	34%
Asians, Europeans, Arabs	1%

Kikuyu schoolchildren

The government encourages the preservation of regional languages. The national radio service broadcasts in more than fifteen African languages. Some radio programs are also broadcast in Hindustani, an Indian dialect.

In villages where all or most of the children have learned the same African language at home, students are taught in that language for the first three grades. They also learn both English and Swahili in primary and secondary schools. English is the language of instruction in high school and university classes. French, German, and Arabic are also offered in schools.

Many Kenyans grow up knowing several languages. Often people mix words from more than one language in casual conversation. A Luhya boy growing up in Nairobi would probably understand and speak four languages by the time he reaches second grade. His parents, who moved here from their ancestral home in Western Province, would have taught him Luhya, his "mother tongue." He might pick up Kikuyu from playmates, Swahili from shopkeepers and other adults, and English from school. Well-educated Kenyan adults often learn one or two additional foreign languages.

Teenagers in Nairobi also have a slang language of their own, just like city kids everywhere. Called "Sheng," it is a mixture of Swahili, English, and other languages.

Swahili is a Bantu language, but over the centuries it has added many words from other languages, especially Arabic. For example, the names of all the numerals between 20 and 1,000 are Arabic, while *laki*, the word for 100,000, is from Hindustani. Another Hindustani word is *chanalua*, meaning "mosquito netting." In Swahili, "money" is either *fedha*, an Arabic word, or *pesa*, originally from the Portuguese. *Daktari* (doctor) and *polisi* (police) are obviously from English.

European missionaries learned Swahili. They used the Latin alphabet to write it, and it is pronounced as it is spelled. Spellings vary a bit, however.

Tribes

There are more than forty different groups in Kenya that are referred to as tribes, or ethnic groups. Definitions of these tribes are blurry, however, and there are numerous subgroups.

Swahili Word List

Visitors and newcomers to Kenya quickly pick up a number of very commonly used words. Here are a few of them:

Jambo.	Hello.
Habari	How are you?
Mzuri.	I'm fine.
Asante.	Thank you.
Bibi	Madam
Bwana	Sir
Rafiki	Friend
Matatu	Bus
Duka	Shop
Soko	Market
Shamba	Cultivated field
Hatari	Danger
Twiga	Giraffe
Simba	Lion

Members of the Njemps tribe

Dancers of the Samburu

Intermarriage is frequent, especially in towns. An ethnic group, according to the dictionary, is a number of people "classed according to common racial, national, tribal, religious, linguistic, or cultural origin or background."

Before colonial times, ethnic groups generally functioned under a council of elders, with no single person at the top. The British governers wanted to deal with leaders, so in some cases they simply decided that a group of related people made up a "tribe." Then they appointed a "chief" and gave him the authority to represent the government.

Friend for Life

One of the most important traditional ceremonies in the lives of many young Kenyan men is circumcision. Circumcision is commonplace among many, but not all, Kenyan ethnic groups. A notable exception is the Luo group. When a good-sized group of young men in a village or community are ready to be recognized as adults, they go through a rite of passage. Each young man is circumcised, and it is important to be brave and not show any pain. For the rest of the young man's life, he has a special relationship with this group, called an "age-group." The closeness age-group members feel is something like that of fraternity brothers.

The Bantu-language groups, by far the most numerous in Kenya, make up about two-thirds of the population. Most of the rest of the groups in Kenya are Nilotic. The Cushitic people, a small minority, occupy the largest part of Kenyan land. For the most part, they live in Kenya's northeastern desert region.

The five largest tribes in population are the the Kikuyu, the Luhya, the Kalenjin, the Luo, and the Kamba. The Kikuyu, the Luhya, and the Kamba are Bantu groups; the Kalenjin and the Luo are Nilotic.

More than 5 million Kenyan people call themselves Kikuyu. This is the largest ethnic group in the nation. Most of them lived in the Central Province at one time, but many have migrated to other parts of Kenya. Many have bought land and continue to work in agriculture,

This market is in a Masai area, but Kikuyu traders run most of the businesses.

The Masai

The Masai (sometimes spelled Maasai), a Nilotic group, are a small minority of Kenya's population. They have been more successful in maintaining the traditions and lifestyle of their ancestors than many other ethnic groups. Europeans often encountered the Masai in early travels to Kenya, and they described them as aggressive and courageous.

Traditionally, the Masai are nomadic herders who move about with the seasons to find adequate water and pastureland for their cattle. Their wealth is measured by the size of their herds. Masai people live in small family clans. As the nomadic way of life becomes harder to sustain, some have banded together to run large ranches. Few of them live in cities, although it is not unusual to see them on the streets or in office buildings in Nairobi or other cities, often dressed in their traditional clothing and wearing elaborate beadwork necklaces and other adornments.

Today, not all of the young Masai become herders when they grow up. Many go away to high school and college. They continue to have close ties with family and members of their age-group, however, and return from time to time to participate in ceremonies.

Some individual Masai work with park personnel to help in the preservation of threatened animal species. A few local Masai settlements allow tourists to visit their villages for a fee. The visitors can talk with the villagers, take photos, and buy souvenirs.

the traditional occupation. Others have gone into business or other professions. The Kikuyu were in the forefront of the struggle for independence.

The Luhya homeland is Western Province, a fertile and well-watered area north of Lake Victoria that is ideal for farming. Luhya are represented in all professions. Unlike the Kikuyu, they have not migrated away from their traditional homeland to any great extent.

The ancestors of the Kalenjin were nomadic cattle herders who settled in the forests and highlands west of the Rift Valley. Today, the Kalenjin practice modern agriculture and are particularly prominent in dairy farming. At one time the Kalenjin were considered to be a group of fairly unconnected tribes, but when President Moi, a Kalenjin, took over as Kenya's second president, those tribes united to form a powerful political force.

Luo fishers on Lake Victoria

The economy and diet of the Luo have always revolved around fish. Their ancestors migrated down the Nile River and settled around Lake Victoria in Kenya and Uganda. After the arrival of the colonists, many Luo left their villages and went to work in places like Mombasa and Nairobi. The Luo played a vital role in the emergence of the trade union movement and, much later, in the struggle for multiparty democracy. Tom Mboya and Oginga Odinga were Luo.

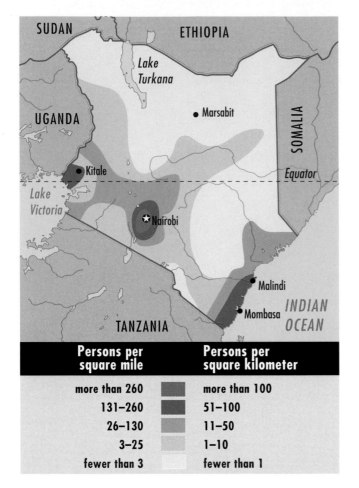

Persons per square mile		Persons per square kilometer
more than 260		more than 100
131–260		51–100
26–130		11–50
3–25		1–10
fewer than 3		fewer than 1

Population of Major Cities (2000 census)

Nairobi	2,143,254
Mombasa	665,018
Kisumu	322,734
Nakuru	231,262
Eldoret	197,449

The Kamba are a predominantly agricultural people living east of Nairobi. Because their homeland is rather dry, they have adopted effective farming methods such as terracing. In 1937, a colonial administrator claimed that the Kamba's area was becoming a desert, but thanks to good land management, the trend has been reversed. Today, the area supports five times as many people as it did then. The Kamba are known for good discipline. Many of them have become soldiers and officers in the army.

The Cushitic people, less numerous than the Bantus and Nilotes, migrated into Kenya from Somalia and Ethiopia in the nineteenth century. They live on both sides of Kenya's borders with those countries. Their ancestors were hunter-gatherers, and today they are herders and farmers. They raise cattle, camels, sheep, and goats. Some of them are fishers who live near Lake Turkana.

Population Explosion

At the beginning of the twenty-first century, Kenya's population is nearly 30 million. The great majority of these people still lived in rural areas, although there is an ongoing heavy migration from the countryside to the major cities.

Rapid population growth causes great problems for the nation. For a long time, the number of people in Kenya was approximately doubling every two decades. It is difficult for the economy to provide enough housing and facilities for schools, transportation, communication, and health care fast enough to take care of this explosion. In addition, there is danger to the natural habitat of Kenya's magnificent wildlife as cities grow bigger and bigger.

El Molo tribespeople at Lake Turkana

Toward the end of the twentieth century, the rate of population growth began to slow down, and the government census taken in 2000 counted somewhat fewer people than had been expected. Two factors evidently caused this change. Family planning had increased in popularity, so that many Kenyan women were having fewer children than in the past. The other cause is a tragic one: a terrible increase in the death rate as a result of the spread of AIDS.

Father of Scouting

The beauty of Kenya's highlands has lured many people from other countries to settle here. One of them was Lord Robert Baden-Powell, who organized the first Boy Scout troop in 1907. Today, millions of children in more than 140 countries are Boy Scouts and Girl Scouts.

Baden-Powell first visited Kenya in 1935 and fell in love with the plains and peaks near Mount Kenya. He said of the little town of Nyeri, "the nearer to Nyeri, the nearer to bliss." Three years later, he and his wife returned to live there until his death in 1941.

Thousands of Kenyan scouts, as well as those from other parts of the world, visit Nyeri to see where their founder lived. The graves of Lord and Lady Powell, in the municipal graveyard, face Mount Kenya.

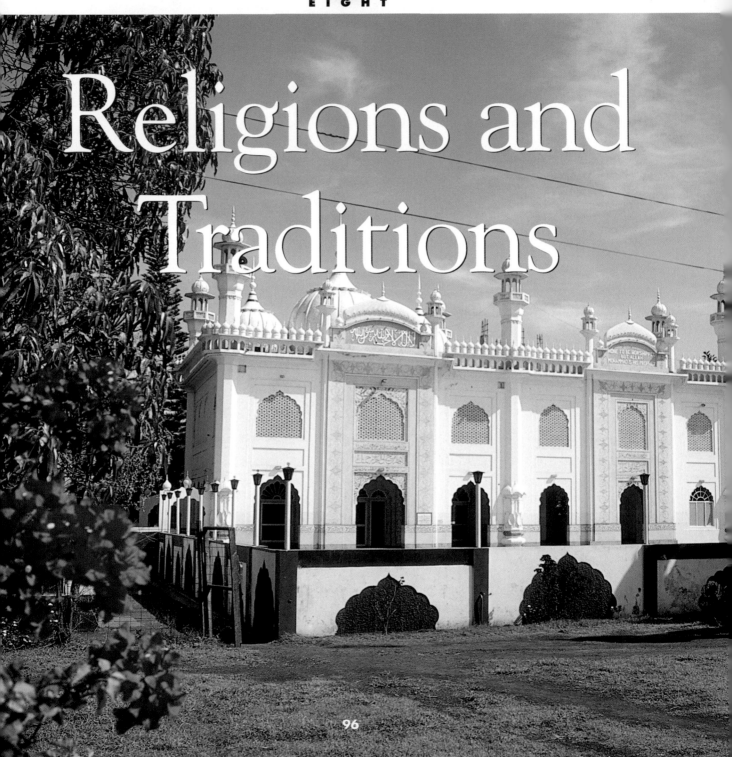

Religions and Traditions

KENYA IS A LAND OF IMMENSE DIVERSITY—IN LANDscape and wildlife, and in the traditions and customs of its people. This diversity extends to religious practices. Houses of worship—cathedrals, chapels, temples, and mosques—are found in the cities and villages of Kenya from the coast to the interior.

Kenya's Constitution guarantees freedom of worship. Students are taught in school that discrimination against any person on the basis of religion is against the national interest.

Major faiths represented in Kenya include Islam, Sikhism, Hinduism, and Christianity of every denomination. There are more than 1,700 registered religious organizations. The majority of the people are Christians; most of the rest practice traditional religions.

Islam was brought to the coast of eastern Africa by Arab travelers in the ninth century A.D. Christian missionaries arrived nearly a thousand years later. Asian immigrants brought their own religions—such as Sikhism and Hinduism— with them.

Opposite: **A mosque welcomes Muslims to worship.**

The beautiful designs on a Hindu temple door

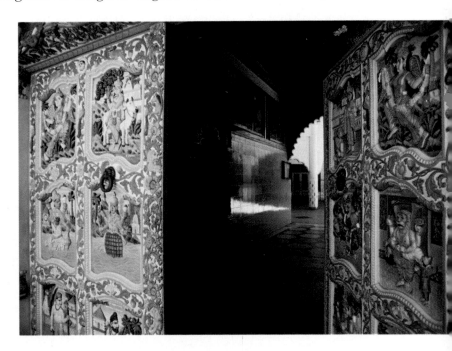

Religions of Kenya

Protestant	38%
Roman Catholic	28%
Traditional beliefs	26%
Muslim	7%
Other	1%

Important Religious Holidays

Good Friday	March or April
Easter	March or April
Id al-Fitr	April (Muslim holiday to mark the end of Ramadan)
Christmas	December 25

A fig tree, sacred in the Kikuya tradition

Traditional Religions

Most early religions throughout the world were forms of animism. This involves the belief that gods or spirits—some good and some evil—live in many elements of nature. In Kenya, traditions and ceremonies differed from one community to another, but there were several common characteristics. These included a belief in one Supreme Creator and the regular offering of prayers. Prayers were said to the spirits of ancestors, who could act as intermediaries with the Supreme God.

There were no priests as such, but wise men—called *laibon* by the Masai—performed rituals to help people through illnesses or other crises. These people represented the force of good against evil. Religious rituals were performed at sacred places, such as particular forests or orchards. Kikuyus would gather under their sacred tree, the fig tree. Some communities believed that God lived in a particular place, such as Mount Kenya or Lake Victoria.

The Masai believe that the rules by which the elders govern were handed down by Masinta, the first Masai. It is believed that God gave him the first gift of cattle. Many wise sayings are attributed to Masinta.

Both Christians and Muslims often retain many of the religious beliefs and customs of their ancestors. Such traditions are important to a people's sense of identity and relationships with one another.

Marriage Customs

Because Kenya is a multicultural society, marriage ceremonies take many forms, all of which are legally recognized. Generally speaking, Hindus, Sikhs, Muslims, and Christians all practice the marriage formalities of their religious faith. In addition, couples can be married in the attorney general's office without a religious service. This is not common in Kenya, and it usually occurs only when the young people's parents have not consented to the union.

A traditional African marriage involves negotiations between the families of the young man and woman. The boy's family will give the girl's family some money, livestock, or other goods. Kenyans call this a "dowry," although it is not the same as the Western definition of a dowry. Sometimes, unfortunately, the girl has no say in the decision. Once the agreements have been reached, the girl moves into the boy's home, where she is welcomed by festivities and rejoicing.

Followers of Islam also go through negotiations and the payment of a dowry. In this case, the payment goes directly to the bride, not to her family. She uses it to buy clothes and basic furnishings for her new home. The Muslim bridegroom goes to the mosque for a religious service, then to the bride's house with a few friends to have dinner. The bride is dressed in finery for the festive family occasion.

Christian marriage ceremonies are similar to those in North America. They are regarded as the final formalization of a marriage, and may not be held until some time after the couple has been married in the traditional way.

Polygamy (when a man has more than one wife) is allowed in both traditional and Muslim families. Christians frown on this practice, but it is not uncommon even among members of Christian churches.

Burial Customs

Burial customs in Kenya differ according to a person's religion and traditions. Hindus and Sikhs are cremated. Muslims are buried in a Muslim cemetery by their fellow Muslims. This is supposed to take place within forty-eight hours after death, which means that a person may be buried far from home. Normally, family members make the arrangements. If no close relatives are nearby at the time of death, Muslim friends take charge.

The body is washed and wrapped in a white shroud. Meanwhile, friends and family gather in another room, where they drink coffee and eat dates. Male friends and relatives then carry the shrouded body to the mosque. After the usual afternoon prayers have been said, the body is placed in the front of the mosque. People say prayers for the deceased person.

Then the body is taken to the cemetery and buried in the shroud only, without a coffin.

Traditional practices among non-Muslims vary widely. Christians hold services at church and prayers at graveside. Most Africans are buried on their own land or on their family's land, not in public cemeteries. Among some groups, the tradition is to invite many people and provide lots of food. Friends and family members help pay the costs of the coffin, the transportation to the burial place, and the feasting, which can be quite high.

Choosing the burial place can sometimes cause family disputes, usually between the widow (or widows, in a polygamous marriage) and elder clan members.

Islam

The religion of Islam, founded in Arabia in A.D. 610 by the prophet Muhammad, teaches the worship of one god, Allah. Arab and Persian traders brought the religion to the coast of

Muslims offer prayers on Id al-Adha, the Feast of Sacrifice.

The Aga Khan Foundation

Ismaili Muslims are led by His Highness Karim Aga Khan IV, believed by his followers to be the direct descendant of the prophet Muhammad. The Aga Khan Foundation has contributed a great deal of money to benefit Kenyans, and many hospitals and schools are named for him.

East Africa 200 years later. Arabs were active in the slave trade, but their religion forbade enslaving a person of the Muslim religion. Partially to avoid slavery, many Africans converted to Islam, which soon became the major religion of the coast. Others became Muslim through intermarriage.

Lamu

By A.D. 1400, there were about forty independent Muslim city-states along the East African coast, most of them on islands or small peninsulas surrounded by mangrove swamps. Each city-state was ruled by a sultan. Their economies were based on trade, with some agriculture and fishing.

Lamu is a small island off the north coast of Kenya, not far from the Somalia border. A visitor to Lamu gets a strong impression of the lifestyle in Arab cities of two and three centuries ago. Most of the buildings in the main part of town date from those times. They are built of white coral or stone, two or three stories high. Rooms are quite narrow because the ceiling beams are made of mangrove poles, and mangroves don't grow very tall. Plasterwork in the rooms is intricately decorated, and Lamu is famous for the beautiful hand-carved wooden front doors that adorn many homes.

No automobiles are permitted on the island except for one belonging to the district commissioner. People use donkeys for transportation up and down the narrow streets and alleys. There are some 10,000 people on Lamu, and about two-thirds as many donkeys. People travel by boat to the mainland, to other islands, and from one part of the island to another.

Virtually all Lamu residents are Muslims.

Muslim Attire

When Muslim women in Kenya go outside, they wear the traditional *bui-bui*. This long, dark cloak covers the hair, flows down over the clothing, and can be pulled across the face to cover everything but the eyes. Inside, in school or at the office, women wear what they choose.

Men often wear a small cap called a *kofia*. On Fridays, the most important day for prayers, they usually put on an ankle-length gown called a *kanzu*.

Muslim law calls for daily prayers and forbids the use of alcoholic beverages. Also, at least once in a lifetime, every devout Muslim who can afford it must make a pilgrimage, or *hajj*, to the holy city of Mecca in Saudi Arabia.

Christianity

The majority of Kenyans are followers of Christianity. Many of the world's mainstream Christian denominations are represented. Included are Roman Catholic, Coptic, Orthodox, Anglican, Friends (Quakers), and many other Protestant groups.

The Portuguese brought Christian ideas to the coast of Kenya in the sixteenth century, but they did not try very hard to spread their religion. Some German missionaries were the first to explore Kenya's interior. They were followed by others from several European countries. The early missionaries encountered several serious problems, but they spread the

Christian philosophy throughout much of the country—except for the Muslim regions—during the colonial period.

A man prays in the Holy Family Catholic Basilica in Nairobi.

The missionaries helped the people of Kenya by establishing schools, building health centers, assisting runaway slaves, and helping to stop the slave trade. They explored and mapped the country, built roads, wrote the first Swahili grammar book and dictionary, and carried out various valuable research projects. Some missionaries helped found cooperatives as a means of improving economic conditions. They also started schools and work projects for disabled people.

But missionaries also undermined some traditional customs and supported the colonial system. Many of them, though they meant well, had paternalistic and racist prejudices. They did little or nothing to oppose the exploitation of Africans by colonial settlers. This led many Kenyans to leave the established churches and form their own independent Christian groups. The National Christian Council of Kenya includes both the independent Christian churches and members of traditional denominations.

Independent Christian Churches

Members who broke away from the missionaries' churches did not want to give up their own traditions. For example, polygamy was a long-established way of life among many

A service at the African Church of the Holy Spirit in Nairobi

groups, and the missionaries tried to stamp out the practice. They also disapproved of using African music in services. In protest, many African groups formed their own churches.

The number of Afro-Christian churches continues to grow. Services in independent churches include drumming, chanting, clapping, and other vigorous expressions of emotion. Members often hold special processionals on Sundays. Carrying colorful banners and wearing symbols of their own denomination—special turbans, robes, and embroidered crosses—they march joyfully down the street drumming, singing, and dancing.

The Afro-Christian churches worked closely with Kenyan political groups during the colonial period. Some of them founded and supported independent African schools and colleges as early as the 1920s.

A procession of Legio Maria Church

C H A P T E R

N I N E

Sports,
the Arts,
and Crafts

KENYANS ARE PASSIONATE ABOUT FOOTBALL—OR SOCCER, as it is called in the United States. They enjoy many sports and games, but none more than football. Young people play it at school and in village parks. Two club teams, Gor Mahia and the AFC Leopards—major rivals in the National Football League—draw huge crowds. The Kenyan National Team, called the Harambee Stars, has won the East and Central African Championship eight times.

Opposite: **A soccer game in Kisumu**

A young soccer player

Rugby, cricket, and volleyball are played in many schools, colleges, and clubs throughout the country. Some companies also sponsor their own teams. Sports clubs have facilities for various activities, including golf, tennis, squash, lawn bowling, and croquet. There are more than twenty sports clubs in Nairobi alone.

Field hockey has become widely popular since the installation of artificial turf in the City Park Stadium. In 1987, a Kenyan field hockey team won a gold medal in the All-Africa Games.

Major international sporting events are held in the large, ultramodern Moi International Stadium northwest of Nairobi. Horse racing attracts spectators during most of the year at the Ngong Road Racecourse, which is also close to Nairobi.

World Records

Kenyans began winning international championships even before independence, at the 1958 Commonwealth Games. Runner Kipchoge Keino won his first gold medal at the All-Africa Games in 1965. He collected two more the next year at the Commonwealth Games, and his teammate Naftali Temu picked up a third.

At the Olympic Games in Mexico City in 1968, members of the Kenyan team covered themselves with glory in track and field events. In all, Kenyans won two bronze medals, four silvers, and three golds. Keino and Temu were both gold medalists. Since that year, Kenyans have won more than 40 Olympic medals, five of them at the summer games in Korea in 1988.

Kip Keino

Kipchoge "Kip" Keino (at right, above), born in 1940, started running while working as a policeman. He represented the police in many competitions, and almost always won. In 1962, he left his job to concentrate on athletics. Over the next eleven years, Kip broke many world records, attained fame and fortune, and was greatly adored by his fellow citizens.

But Keino wanted to do more with his life than break records. For many years, he felt he couldn't enjoy the good life without trying to help the many suffering children in Kenya. He used his own earnings from athletics and raised money from the many friends he had made around the world. He used these funds to establish the Kipchoge Keino Children's Home for homeless youngsters. He and his wife take care of about 80 children on their farm near Eldoret in western Kenya (pictured below). More than 100 others have finished school at the home and gone out on their own. They all regard Kip and Phyllis Keino as their parents.

In 1996, Kip was awarded the Sports Humanitarian Hall of Fame trophy, presented to him by former U.S. president Ronald Reagan. In 1999, he was elected chairman of the National Olympic Committee of Kenya. Later, he also became a member of the International Olympic Committee.

At the end of 1998, Kenyan runners held seven world records. Interestingly, nearly all of Kenya's athletic stars come from the Great Rift Valley region.

Kenyans are frequent winners in marathon races held in London, New York, Honolulu, and Boston. In April 2000, Kenyan men won three of the first four places in the Boston Marathon. Catherine Ndereba came in first among women,

Marathon winner Catherine Ndereba

and is now known affectionately as "Catherine the Great." In October 2000, Kenya won the World Youth Athletics Championship in Santiago, Chile, by bagging fourteen medals, seven of them gold.

Mombasa hosts a marathon of its own each July.

Music and Drama Festivals

Music, dance, and storytelling have been a part of Kenyan culture for generations. Many Kenyan children are taught to perform in public at an early age. In school, youngsters learn to sing and recite traditional songs and stories, often in a different language than the one they speak at home. They use these skills to perform for various festive occasions.

Schoolchildren perform traditional dances.

Bomas of Kenya

A large tourist attraction—and a center of Kenyan cultural activities—is called Bomas of Kenya. It is located near the main gates of Nairobi National Park. *Boma* is a Swahili word for an enclosed homestead. Visitors can tour bomas that represent several of Kenya's major ethnic groups, buy traditional crafts, and watch ethnic dance programs in a large circular theater. The Bomas Harambee Dancers, a resident professional dance company, perform daily. They are accompanied by drums and other traditional instruments.

The British colonial government founded the Kenya Music Festival, which is still an important activity in schools. Competitions are held at the district, provincial, and national levels. Soloists, small groups, and large choirs compete in different age categories. Western, African, and Asian music—as well as poetry recitals in various languages—are included in the program.

The Schools and Colleges Drama Festival operates much like the Kenya Music Festival. Most of the plays are written by students and teachers. National winners of the competition are invited to perform for the president. The Schools and Colleges Drama Festival also includes a Cultural Dance category, in which traditional scenes are depicted in dance.

Audiences who watch finalists perform in these festivals are thrilled at the quality of the presentations, and the experiences enrich the lives of those who take part for many years afterward. Many of the performers continue to be active in theatrical groups as adults.

Performing Arts

Nairobi has its own symphony orchestra and a repertory theater, called the Phoenix Players. Performing artists from all over the world include a stop in Nairobi in their schedules. Many Kenyans are members of choirs. The Muugano National Choir, directed by Boniface Mganga, is famous. It has performed in many countries around the world and has made a number of recordings. Kenyan singers, instrumentalists, and songwriters are active in the field of popular entertainment. The song "Malaika," written by Fadhili Williams, was made popular by Harry Belafonte.

Movies

Quite a few movies have been shot in Kenya. One of them, *Out of Africa*, lured thousands of tourists to Kenya to see the beautiful landscape and the wildlife for themselves.

Scene from the movie
Out of Africa

The Work of Two Women

When award-winning movie director Anne Mungai was asked by UNICEF (United Nations International Children's Emergency Fund) to make two films about street children in Kenya, she didn't know what the consequences would be. She asked her actress friend Anne Wanjugu to help with the project.

The two women grew to love the street children they met. They decided to set up a home for the kids, and Anne Wanjugu became the housemother. There, the children learn useful trades, and they also take part in a theatrical troupe. Admission fees to their performances help to pay the costs of the home.

A hand-carved wooden door

Local children are often used in foreign-produced films. Edwin Mahinda, a seventh-grader when he starred in *Kitchen Toto*, has appeared in several other movies since then. Many other Kenyan boys have also won movie roles. Jack Kariuki played a slave boy in *Out of Darkness*, Adam Osman appeared in *Wildlands*, and Collins Muthupi was in *Cheetah and the Hare*.

Arts and Crafts

Kenya has a strong arts and crafts tradition. When Europeans first came to the coast of Kenya, they found Swahili people living in fine two-story houses in towns. Their thick doors were beautifully and ornately carved, as were many pieces of wooden furniture. Decorated plasterwork appeared in many rooms. Women were wearing locally crafted gold and silver jewelry.

In order to preserve these traditional arts, the National Museums of Kenya has set up training programs for young people in Mombasa and Lamu. Historic areas in the two towns are protected from change. Many trained students find employment restoring old coastal houses. Hand-carved doors and furniture from Lamu can be seen in public buildings throughout the country.

Many items handmade in Kenya are exported to other countries. Hand-carved animals are especially popular. Pottery, baskets, leather goods, and items made of soapstone

A couple sell Kenyan crafts.

(chess sets, for example) can be found in gift shops and import stores. Handwoven clothing and garments made of batik or tie-dyed materials have a typically African look. Tourists also like to buy Masai-made spears, shields, necklaces, and earrings.

Elimo Njau is an artist who has done a great deal to encourage Kenyan artists. At the time of independence, he gained wide recognition as a painter for a series of murals that portrayed the Nativity in an African context. Later, he

Kitengela Stained Glass

An artist named Nani Croze founded the Kitengela Stained Glass Studios in 1970. She now has several dozen employees who work with her in the production of stained-glass panels and blown-glass art objects.

Croze found it difficult to import colored glass, so she experimented with recycled bottles and window glass. Making a stained glass panel involves rolling, cutting, painting, and firing the glass several times before the final process of leading and cementing the pieces into finished panels.

Artworks from Kitengela Studios appear in many Kenyan hospitals, offices, banks, and churches.

founded the Paa ya Paa Cultural Center, where artists came from all parts of the world to paint and sculpt. Many of their works, as well as those by Njau himself, were displayed there.

Cultural events such as poetry readings and seasonal celebrations were held at the center. In 1997, tragedy struck when a fire destroyed the center and its art treasures. Njau has not given up, however. Reconstruction of the center is underway, made possible by funds contributed by many well-wishers.

Njau encourages artists to find their own way to express themselves. The motto of the Paa ya Paa Cultural Center is "Do not copy—copying puts God to sleep."

Literature, both English and Swahili, is studied by Kenyan schoolchildren. They also learn about the folklore and traditions of their ancestors through oral literature. Students are encouraged to write their own poetry and read their work at public events.

One of Kenya's best-known authors is Ngugi wa Thiongo. He has written a number of books in English and Kikuyu and has gained an international reputation. Thiongo is currently teaching in the United States.

David Maillu is one of the country's most prolific writers. He has produced more than forty books for both adults and children.

Marjorie Oludhe has also written several dozen novels, as well as poems. A winner of literary awards, she was born in England, is married to a Luo, and has lived in Kenya for forty-five years. Mrs. Asenath Odaga has written several children's books, such as *Jande's Ambition* and *The Secret of Monkey Rock*. Henry Ole Kulet, a Masai, has written about changing lifestyles in Kenya. *To Become a Man* is about a young man caught between the traditional Masai lifestyle and modern society.

Other current writers who are well known in Kenya are Yusuf Dawood, Sam Kahiga, Wahome Mutati, Meja Mwagi, and Margaret Ogola.

A schoolgirl recites a poem.

CHAPTER

TEN

Daily
Activities

118

HOW DO KENYAN CHILDREN SPEND THEIR DAYS? IT depends on many factors, of course, just as it does in any other country. Do they live in the country or in the city? In the desert, on a farm, or at the seacoast? Do they have to work in order to help the family get by? Are they able to go to school?

Opposite: **A Turkana child herds goats to pasture.**

Schools in Kenya

Kenyan children learn many of the same subjects as the ones taught in other countries. Classes in history and geography, naturally, concentrate on their own country. Subjects are taught in English in the upper classes, but all children also learn Swahili.

Fourth graders at a school for girls

Pupils must pass standard examinations in order to be promoted to higher levels in school. The British introduced this program, and the Kenyan government continues it. Teachers use a great deal of repetition in the classroom, to help the pupils learn the facts that will be emphasized in the exams. Because the schools have very little

Mancala

Perhaps you have seen a game called Mancala in a toy store. Maybe you have played it. Most Kenyans grow up playing this game; it is probably the most popular children's game in the nation.

Variations of the game have been played since ancient times in many parts of Africa and Asia. The rules and the shape of the board differ from one region to another, but the principle is the same.

Two players face each other with a board between them. The board is carved into two lines of indentations, or cups. Four pebbles are placed in each cup to start. Then the players take turns moving their pebbles around the board, following rules that allow them to capture their opponent's pieces. The game is over when one player runs out of pebbles. The person with the largest number of them is declared the winner.

Kenyan children call the game *mbao*, which means "board." They don't have to buy this game in a store. Adults or older children in the community carve the board, and ordinary pebbles can be used for the movable pieces.

money, supplies and equipment are in short supply. Science teachers have to be very imaginative; they need to construct most of their own equipment for experiments.

Each school has a uniform—blouse and skirt or dress for girls and shirt and pants for boys, all in specified colors. Most children feel proud to wear the clothes that represent their school.

The government's goal is to provide free schools for all the children in Kenya, but at the present there simply isn't enough money to go around. Unfortunately, some children are not able to go to school at all. Even if there is a school available that doesn't charge any fees, some people can't afford to buy books and uniforms for their children. In spite of problems, the government has managed to make some progress in education for both children and adults.

National Holidays in Kenya	
New Year's Day	January 1
Labor Day	May 1
Madaraka Day (Self-rule)	June 1
Kenyatta Day (anniversary of the day Kenyatta was arrested)	October 10
Jamhuri Day (Independence/Republic Day)	December 12

Wildlife Clubs

More than 50,000 Kenyans, most of them schoolchildren, belong to the Wildlife Clubs of Kenya (WCK). Clubs are formed in the schools and are registered with the Kenya Wildlife Service (KWS). Members pay a small fee, which allows them free entrance to all KWS areas and parks. Clubs go on organized trips to view wildlife. They also take part in projects, such as taking care of animals and making bird feeders and aquariums.

The Wildlife Clubs are an important part of the lives of

People learn about the environment at a study center.

Kenyan Names

Most Kenyans use three names—a given African name, their father's name, and, if they are Christian, a Christian name. For example, a Kikuyu boy might be called John Kamau Kimani. John is his Christian name, Kamau is his given name, and Kimani is the name of his father. The given name is chosen before birth, but a Christian name may not be added until the child is baptized. Muslim names follow a similar tradition.

Given names differ among ethnic groups. Kikuyu traditions for naming children after relatives are quite rigid. The first child is named for the father's father or mother, the second child is named for the wife's father or mother, other children are named after uncles, and so on. Luo names sometimes stand for the time of birth, with such meanings as "born at night," or "born when it is raining." Among the Luhya, elderly members of the family choose the name of a new baby. Usually the name is that of a deceased relative. Nicknames are common. Some people encourage their friends to use these instead of the names they are given at birth.

many Kenyan children. They participate in activities and celebrate with regional rallies, which are held every year. Thousands of people gather at these rallies to watch parades and take part in the entertainment.

WCK was organized in 1968. Richard Leakey was one of the founders and the first chairman of the board. These clubs have been a major influence in educating Kenyans about the precious asset they have in their wildlife. Many adult Kenyans working in wildlife and conservation projects are former WCK members.

Health Care

Public health is a major concern of the Kenyan government. During the first couple of decades of independence, statistics showed declines in the death rate and infant mortality rate. There were improvements in health education, sanitation, provision of clean water, and immunizations. The country

The Flying Doctors

The Flying Doctors' Society of Africa (FDSA) is a membership organization that has provided many heroic and dramatic rescue services. When notice comes in of a person injured or taken ill while stranded in a remote area, the FDSA takes to the air, ready to deliver life-saving supplies, equipment, and expertise to the victim. Nurses and pilots perform emergency procedures and rush the patients to a hospital.

FDSA performed 517 evacuations during 1999. In 1991, the service rescued 26 people in a single day.

Their airborne adventures have included quite a few crash landings, but none of the crashes has resulted in loss of life.

FDSA shares an address with a sister organization, the African Medical and Research Foundation (AMREF). AMREF's doctors have performed amazing feats of reconstructive surgery on severely injured or deformed patients. The organization is active in health education in schools and training of health personnel. Its motto is "Health for All in Africa."

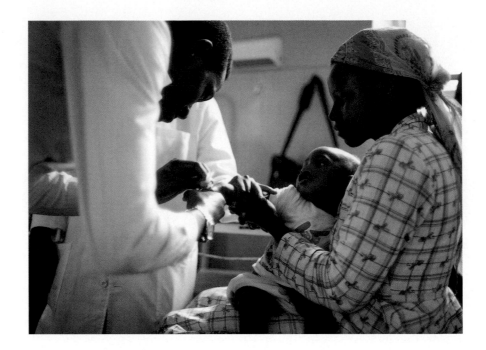

Doctors immunize infants and children at a hospital in Nairobi.

continues to suffer a shortage of doctors and dentists, but there have been increases in the numbers of nurses and midwives.

Food

What do Kenyans eat? Kenya's ideal climate and long growing season provide a wide variety of vegetables and fruits. Kenyan farms produce vegetables for export to Europe. Children grow up eating bananas, mangoes, papayas, pineapples, and many other fruits.

Kenyans eat almost no canned or frozen foods. Everything is prepared fresh daily. A family's meal commonly consists of a starch such as ugali, chapatis, or rice, along with vegetables. If they can afford it, the family might also eat a meat or fish stew. Rice cooked with coconut milk and fish is popular in coastal areas.

Vegetables and fruits for sale in a market

Common Kenyan Dishes

Ugali	Cooked white maize (corn) meal
Chapatis	Flat, round, unleavened bread (Indian origin)
Mandazi	Deep-fried triangular pastry, usually a little sweet
Samosa	Pastry turnover filled with meat or vegetables
Githeri	Maize and beans
Matoke	Cooked green bananas or plantains (Ugandan word)
Kienyeji	Vegetables, beans, and potatoes mashed together
Uji	Porridge, usually of millet
Sukuma wiki	Kale

A street vendor selling roasted corn

For festive occasions, the favorite food is *nyama choma*—roast meat, or barbecue. At outdoor places where construction crews or office workers gather at lunchtime, women prepare and serve popular foods.

Common snack foods are samosas, mandazis, and peanuts, but the most popular snack is a piece of roasted corn, sold by street vendors. Kenyan children, just like kids in many other countries, love french fries—which they call "chips."

The Twenty-First Century

Kenya is a young nation. At the start of this century, it was just thiry-six years old. It had gone through a huge change, from a colony run by a foreign power to an independent nation with a government elected by the Kenyan people.

The vast majority of Kenya's citizens are also young. As the years go by, fewer and fewer of them remember much about colonial days. They are more interested in current national and international affairs than in following traditions of the past. Kenya's young people are keenly aware of the problems the nation faces, such as widespread poverty and the frightening spread of AIDS. They are also full of hope, strong opinions, and creative ideas about solutions to these problems.

What is Kenya? It is an awe-inspiring landscape, home to millions of magnificent animals and birds. It is a country of wide open spaces, quiet villages, and large, energetic cities. It is most of all a multicultural, multireligious, multiracial nation whose people have faith in their ability to pull together to create a bright future.

Timeline

Kenya History

Early ancestors of mankind are living in Kenya.	**About 2,000,000 B.C.**
Homo sapiens are living in Kenya.	**About 15,000– 3000 B.C.**
Islamic Arabs begin trading on Kenya's coast.	A.D. 900
A Swahili town is founded in present-day Gedi.	1400
Vasco da Gama arrives from Portugal in present-day Malindi.	1498
Portuguese build Fort Jesus in Mombasa.	1593
The Portuguese leave Kenya.	1729
Britain and Germany partition East Africa, with Britain gaining control over Kenya.	1886
The British government begins to build a railroad from Mombasa to Kisumu.	1896

World History

2500 B.C.	Egyptians build the Pyramids and Sphinx in Giza.
563 B.C.	Buddha is born in India.
A.D. 313	The Roman emperor Constantine recognizes Christianity.
610	The prophet Muhammad begins preaching a new religion called Islam.
1054	The Eastern (Orthodox) and Western (Roman) Churches break apart.
1066	William the Conqueror defeats the English in the Battle of Hastings.
1095	Pope Urban II proclaims the First Crusade.
1215	King John seals the Magna Carta.
1300s	The Renaissance begins in Italy.
1347	The Black Death sweeps through Europe.
1453	Ottoman Turks capture Constantinople, conquering the Byzantine Empire.
1492	Columbus arrives in North America.
1500s	The Reformation leads to the birth of Protestantism.
1776	The Declaration of Independence is signed.
1789	The French Revolution begins.
1865	The American Civil War ends.

Kenya History

Nairobi becomes the capital of the colony of Kenya.	1907
The Crown Lands Ordinance declares that only white people can own land.	1915
Kenya is renamed the Kenya Colony and Protectorate.	1920
Harry Thuku founds the Young Kikuyu Association (YKA).	1921
Jomo Kenyatta pleads for the rights of Indians and Africans in East Africa.	1929
Kenyatta becomes president of the Kenya African Union (KAU).	1947
British-trained Kenyan ex-soldiers form the Mau Mau army and lead raids on anyone loyal to the British government.	1948
The British governor calls a state of emergency in Kenya.	1952–1957
Kenya becomes an independent nation, with Kenyatta as president.	1963
At the Olympic Games in Mexico City, Kenya's team wins medals.	1968
Daniel arap Moi succeeds to the presidency on Kenyatta's death.	1978
Members of Kenyan's Air Force unsuccessfully try to overthrow Moi.	1982
The first multiparty elections are held in Kenya.	1992
An economic crisis begins that lasts through the 1990s.	1993
Terrorists bomb the U.S. embassy in Nairobi, killing more than 250 people; Kenyan runners hold seven world records.	1998
Kenyans win three of the first four places in the Boston Marathon.	2000

World History

1914	World War I breaks out.
1917	The Bolshevik Revolution brings Communism to Russia.
1929	Worldwide economic depression begins.
1939	World War II begins, following the German invasion of Poland.
1945	World War II ends.
1957	The Vietnam War starts.
1969	Humans land on the moon.
1975	The Vietnam War ends.
1979	Soviet Union invades Afghanistan.
1983	Drought and famine in Africa.
1989	The Berlin Wall is torn down, as Communism crumbles in Eastern Europe.
1991	Soviet Union breaks into separate states.
1992	Bill Clinton is elected U.S. president.
2000	George W. Bush is elected U.S. president.

Fast Facts

Official name: Republic of Kenya

Capital: Nairobi

Official languages: Swahili and English

Nairobi

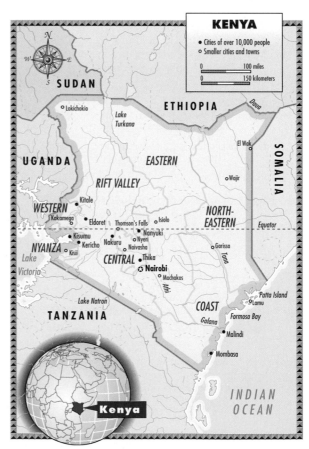

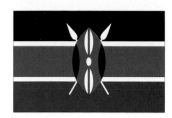
Kenya's flag

Thomson's Falls

Official religion:	None
Year of founding:	1963
National anthem:	*Ee Mungu Nguvu Yetu* ("Oh God of All Creation")
Government:	Republic
Chief of state:	President
Head of government:	President
Area:	224,979 square miles (582,650 sq km)
Dimensions:	640 miles (1,030 km) north to south; 560 miles (901 km) east to west
Coordinates of geographic center:	1°0' N, 38°0' E
Land and water borders:	Uganda to the west, Tanzania to the south, the Indian Ocean and Somalia to the east, Ethiopia to the north, Sudan to the northwest
Highest elevation:	Mount Kenya, 17,058 feet (5,199 m) above sea level
Lowest elevation:	Sea level along the coast of the Indian Ocean
Average temperature extremes:	54°F (12°C) in Nairobi at night in January; 81°F (27°C) in Kisumu during the day in July
Average precipitation extremes:	10 inches (25 cm) in the north; 70 inches (178 cm) in the elevated eastern area of the Lake Victoria basin
National population (2000 census):	28,686,607

Great Rift Valley

Population of largest cities (2000 census):

Nairobi	2,143,254
Mombasa	665,018
Kisumu	322,734
Nakuru	231,262
Eldoret	197,449

Famous landmarks:
- ▶ *Aberdare National Park,* in the central highlands
- ▶ *Amboseli National Reserve,* southern Kenya
- ▶ *Fort Jesus,* in Mombasa
- ▶ *Great Rift Valley*
- ▶ *Lake Victoria,* in western Kenya
- ▶ *Masai Mara National Reserve,* on the border with Tanzania
- ▶ *Mount Kenya,* in the central highlands
- ▶ *Nairobi National Park,* in southern Kenya
- ▶ *Parliament building,* in Nairobi

Industry: Nairobi and Mombasa are Kenya's main industrial centers. Petroleum from other countries is refined in Mombasa. Food processing is Kenya's main industry. Other important industries are manufacturing of machinery, paper goods, and textiles. Kenya's main mining activities involve soda ash, fluorspar, and salt.

Currency

Currency: Kenya's monetary unit is the Kenyan shilling (K Sh), which equals 100 cents. In mid-2001, U.S.$1 = 79.30 K Sh.

System of weights and measures: Metric system

Literacy rate: 78 percent

Kikuyu children

Jomo Kenyatta

Common Swahili words and phrases:

Asante. (ah-SAN-tay)	Thank you.
Habari gani? (Ha-BAH-re GAH-nee)	What's new? *or* How are you?
Harambee. (ha-RAAM-bay)	Let's pull together.
Jambo. (JAHM-bo)	Hello.
Lala salama. (LA-la sa-LAHM-ah)	Good night *or* sleep well
Ngapi? (en-GAH-pi)	How much?
Ngoja! (en-GOH-jah)	Wait!
nzuri (en-ZUR-I)	good
Saa ngapi? (SAH-ah en-GAH-pi)	What time is it?
uhuru (oo-HOO-roo)	independence *or* freedom

Famous Kenyans:

Joy Adamson (1910–1980)
Wildlife conservationist, author

Kipchoge "Kip" Keino (1940–)
Athlete

Jomo Kenyatta (ca. 1895–1978)
Freedom fighter, president

Louis Leakey (1903–1972)
Scientist

Mary Leakey (1913–1996)
Scientist

Richard Leakey (1944–)
Conservationist, scientist

Daniel arap Moi (1924–)
President

Tom Mboya (1930–1969)
Political leader

Harry Thuku (?–1970)
Political organizer

To Find Out More

Fiction

▶ Anderson, Joy. *Juma and the Magic Jinn*. New York: Lothrop, Lee & Shepard Books, 1986.

▶ Mbabu, Elisha. *From Home Guard to Mau Mau*. Nairobi: East African Educational Publishers, 1996.

▶ Smith, Roland. *Thunder Cave*. New York: Hyperion Books for Children, 1997.

▶ Several books published by Wildlife Clubs of Kenya can be ordered from
Book Service by Post
P.O. Box 29, Douglas
Isle of Man IM99 IBQ
E-mail: bookshop@enterprise.net

Nonfiction

▶ Adamson, Joy. *Born Free*. Cutchogue, N.Y.: Buccaneer Books, 1994.

▶ Neimark, Anne E. *Wild Heart: The Story of Joy Adamson, Author of Born Free*. San Diego: Harcourt, 1999.

▶ Spoerry, Anne. *They Call Me Mama Daktari*. Norval, Ontario: Moulin Publishing, 1997.

▶ Visram, M.G. *Allidina Visram, the Trail Blazer*. Mombasa, Kenya: M.G. Visram, 1990.

▶ Wepman, Dennis. *Jomo Kenyatta*. Broomall, Pa.: Chelsea House Publishers, 1985.

Websites

▶ **Kenyaweb.com**
http://www.kenyaweb.com
Extensive collection of information about Kenya

▶ **National Museums of Kenya**
http://www.museums.or.ke
The arts and culture of Kenya; includes photo galleries and links to regional museums.

▶ **Daily Nation**
http://www.nationaudio.com
A Kenyan newspaper, with selections from each day's news

Organizations and Embassies

▶ **Kenya Embassy**
2249 R Street, NW
Washington, D.C. 20008
(202) 387-6101

▶ **Kenya Wildlife Service**
P.O. Box 40241
Nairobi, Kenya
http://www.kws.org/

Index

Page numbers in *italics* indicate illustrations.

Meet the Authors

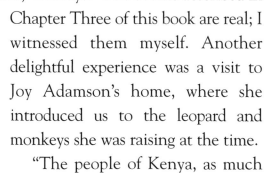

Sylvia McNair has always been interested in other countries. Born in Korea, where her American parents were missionaries, she grew up in Vermont and graduated from Oberlin College. For more than thirty years, she has written and edited books and magazine articles, most of them about travel. More than twenty of her books have been published by Children's Press.

McNair's interest in Kenya started when her niece, Lynne Mansure, went there to live. She has made several visits to the country. "There is no greater thrill than going on a safari to view Kenya's magnificent animals," she says. "The events described in Chapter Three of this book are real; I witnessed them myself. Another delightful experience was a visit to Joy Adamson's home, where she introduced us to the leopard and monkeys she was raising at the time.

"The people of Kenya, as much as the wildlife, have made those visits unforgettable for me. So many Kenyans helped us gather materials for this book."

L YNNE MANSURE is the author of several books for children, including *Mystery in Lamu*, an exciting story about children who helped to track down some poachers. She is also a frequent contributor to Kenyan newspapers. Mansure's parents were missionaries in Zimbabwe (then Rhodesia). She spent most of her childhood there before returning to the United States for her high school and college education.

"During my years at Earlham College and later on at the Sorbonne in Paris, I always wanted to go back to Africa," Mansure says. "When the opportunity came to teach French in Kenya, I jumped at it." She taught for a number of years, then was named inspector of schools. In this capacity, she supervised schools throughout Kenya.

The collaboration between McNair and Mansure could not have been accomplished efficiently without the use of e-mail. Drafts of chapters sped electronically back and forth between McNair's home in Evanston, Illinois, and Mansure's home in a suburb of Nairobi, Kenya. "As we got close to finishing the book, we were exchanging long e-mails almost every day."

Some unavoidable delays occurred when a serious shortage of water resulted in electricity rationing in Nairobi. Sometimes Mansure could use her computer only during the night; at other times there was a total blackout in her area for several days. "But both of us were so interested in our subject matter, this collaboration was a great experience in spite of the difficulties," says McNair.

Photo Credits